To Nancy . . . with love

Mitch & Margot Reardon

ZULULAND

a wildlife heritage

C. STRUIK PUBLISHERS CAPE TOWN

Published by C. Struik (Pty) Ltd
Struik House
Oswald Pirow Street
Foreshore
Cape Town

First edition: 1984
Copyright © Mitch & Margot Reardon
Design by Martin Field, Cape Town
Typeset by McManus Bros (Pty) Ltd, Cape Town
Lithographic reproduction by
Hirt & Carter (Pty) Ltd., Cape Town
Printed and bound by
Tien Wah Press (Pte) Ltd, Singapore

ISBN 0 86977 193 0

The following extracts are reproduced by kind
permission of the authors, publishers or editors: the
verse from the poem *I Heard the Old Songs* by B. W.
Vilakazi from *The Penguin Book of South African
Verse*, edited by Jack Cope and Uys Krige, copyright
to Witwatersrand University Press; the description of
the dog baboon, Chapter 6 is from *Territorial
Imperative* by Robert Ardrey and copyright to
William Collins and Son, London; extracts from
Shaka's Country by T. V. Bulpin is copyright to
Hodder and Stoughton, Sevenoaks, Kent. The quote
about the Abatwa people in Chapter 7 is from *African
Beginnings* by Olivia Vlahos, Viking Penguin Inc.,
New York; the habitat behaviour of the palmnut
vulture in Chapter 8 is from the *Red Data Book*,
published by Aves, 1976.

CONTENTS

ACKNOWLEDGEMENTS

We are greatly indebted to the Director and staff of the Natal
Parks Board, whose friendly co-operation was so essential to
the success of this book. In particular we would like to thank
Dr John Vincent who smoothed the way and offered
constructive advice and Tony and Barbara Tomkinson who
were most helpful in innumerable ways, not the least of
which was the hospitality of their home at St Lucia. In
gratitude for information, assistance and kindness we
mention the following knowing that the names of others no
less helpful will occur when it is too late: Brian O'Regan,
Richard Emslie, Simon Pillinger and Khishwanqani
Hlatshwayo (Umfolozi); Tony Wately (Hluhluwe); Mark
Astrup and the 'old man', (Mkuzi); Eddie Harris (Bhanga
Nek); Garnet Jackson (Ndumu); Herb Bourne (Ulundi); Ed
Ostrosky, Andries Malwane (Sihangwane); John Smith
(Mtubatuba); Ted and Liz Reilly (Mlilwane); Mo and Glynis
Penn (Durban); and Leon and Dianne Pappas for their much
appreciated support during the malaria crisis. We thank
Professor John Hanks and Dr Jeremy Grimsdell of the
Institute of Natural Resources in Pietermaritzburg and
Dr Norman Owen-Smith of the University of the Witwaters-
rand, who generously gave of their time and expertise.
Special thanks to Struik's team for providing a happy
combination of warmth and professionalism, in particular
our editor Peggy Jennings and designer Martin Field.

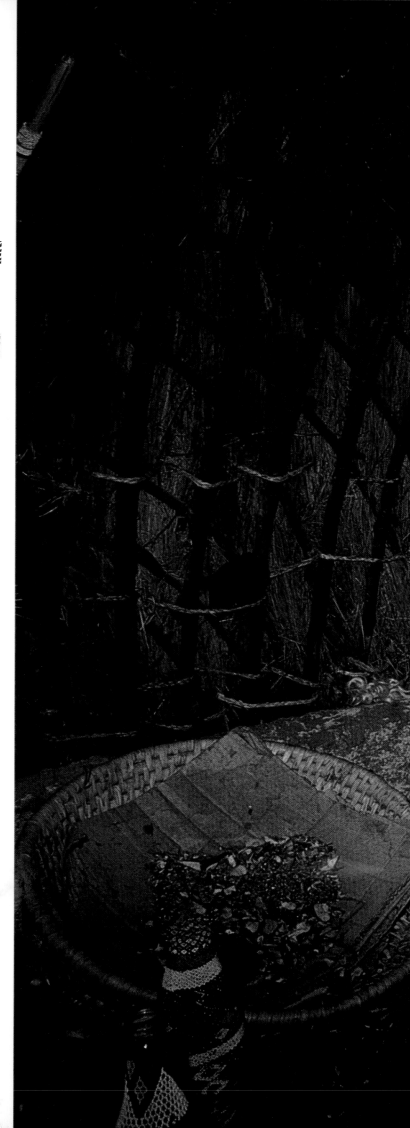

*Prophesying the future, a Zulu 'sangoma' or diviner throws an
assortment of animal knuckle bones and shells while her
apprentice, daubed with white ochre proclaiming her novice
status, looks on. Diviners are said to have the power of prophesy.*

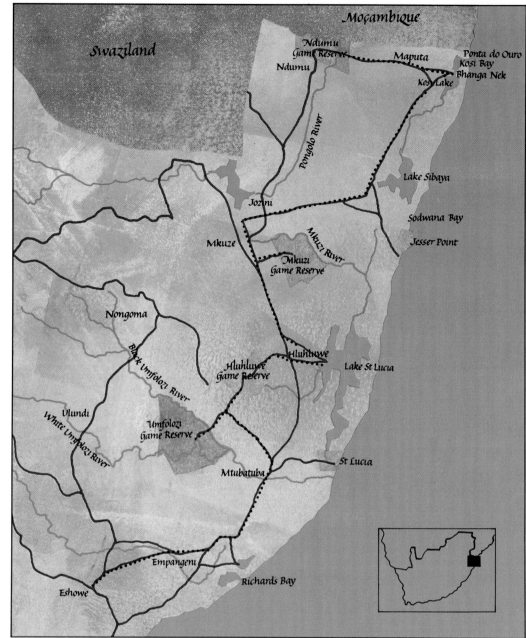

This map of northern Natal and northern KwaZulu indicates the route Mitch and Margot Reardon followed northwards through some of old Zululand in search of the past.

Female cheetah and sub-adult cubs, Umfolozi

PREFACE

My romance with Zululand began in my childhood. Over 17 years, in spite of a long separation, I have retained an interest in its welfare and an abiding love for the people and the country: the strong, unaffected Zulus and their formal, shy children; the forests, bushveld and wild coastline; the buffalo and antelope herds, baboons and rhinos; and also the Whites, farmers and gamerangers, so expediently dismissed by the outside world as settlers and expendable.

Zululand. The name conjures up images – a battlefield, a hunting ground, a home. It also suggests boldness, wilderness, even savagery. The essence of the country was all these things but the seemingly least appropriate description was the truest – old Zululand was fragile. Today much of it has already disappeared under the gun, the axe and the plough.

My return had the quality of a renewed love affair, with all the hope, longing, sweetness and disillusionment that involvement implies. The experience was one of striking contrasts. On the one hand, in Zululand's magnificent game parks and wild places I was privy to scenes out of very earliest Africa, scenes of such composure and haunting beauty as to seem whispers from a paradisiacal age. On the other, beyond the protection of park boundaries, overcrowding has created tableaux of devastation, of land so badly abused as to hold out almost no hope of recovery. The change was from the sublime to the deeply disturbing, but it permitted me to see for myself what all of Zululand had once been like, what had come to pass, and what was now being done to safeguard this wounded proud land.

In that regard Zululand is a microcosm of the rest of Africa, indeed of the entire developing world, where explosively expanding human populations bring intolerable pressures to bear on finite natural resources. Although solutions are elusive, researchers of various disciplines are seeking them. Their findings could well become blueprints for the rest of Africa.

In the old days I found a composite that, although not perfect, appeared to work. There was mutual respect and a sense of history. Whites spoke Zulu as a second tongue and all lived their lives removed from the rude stirrings of the outside world. But subsequent events washed over them and ultimately bore them along. Today they find themselves cast up, stunned and apprehensive, wondering how best to cope. Radicals from persuasions left and right offering horrifying solutions that were unthinkable only a few years ago are now attracting audiences. If calmness and pragmatism should once more prevail it will be against all odds. But Zululand has confounded its critics before, and as before there are men of courage and goodwill wrestling to salvage the situation.

MITCH REARDON
Skukuza, 1984

THE LEOPARD

'Drink one of Africa's waters and you will return to drink again.'

Arab proverb

I was seven years old when my family came to live in Zululand. My father joined my grandfather in establishing the territory's first tyre vulcanizing plant in the tiny capital, Eshowe. Having served as an officer in the New Zealand Navy during World War II he was entitled to a land grant available to ex-servicemen and used it to acquire a plot near the Dlinza forest, within the borough of Eshowe, and built a house there.

Eshowe, a Zulu name describing the sighing of the wind as it plays amongst the trees, is in the highlands, cooler and healthier than the surrounding low country, and was favoured by the Zulu aristocracy in the old days as their place of residence. Chaka's kraal at Bulawayo, 'a vast pattern of several thousand huts, full two miles in circumference, lying on a gentle slope, with a superb view over the immense and misty beauty of the valley of the Mhlathuze' had existed 130 years ago only 30 kilometres from our house. Even closer had been the great military kraal ruled over by Dingane's mother at Kangela on the ridge between Eshowe and Chaka's Bulawayo.

Much had changed since and although it was still, for the most part, undeveloped country when we first arrived, even then the great forests were under siege and big game was very scarce. We had arrived at the end of an era, though that realization only came with hindsight and did not influence our immediate priorities. In the wake of the post-war boom, flux and transition were the order of the day; progress came crowding in and with it old systems were disrupted. It was a burgeoning time with few questions asked, a time to throw off the dreadful war years, to build a new secure future and with its treasurehouse of natural gifts, this was the country to do it in.

What remained of the Dlinza forest was protected by legislation from further desecration and its evergreen interior sheltered troops of black-faced vervet monkeys and sounders of bush pigs; bushbuck and tiny antelope known as blue duiker lived in the shadows while brilliant butterflies and loeries illumined its muted pristine spaces. There was no better place for a boy to grow up in and I looked around this jungle garden with an owner's eye, unaware that it was I who was possessed.

Twice a day I passed through the forest on the way to and from school and in my free time explored its trails in the company of my younger brother Lindsay and a small shaggy golden mongrel named Kerry.

My brother and I stalked the evanescent duiker with homemade bows and arrows without ever putting them at risk. Kerry's job was to bring them to bay but they easily eluded him and the only time he managed to draw alongside, his quarry turned in its tracks and bowled him over with short effective horns. Crestfallen, he limped back, ears drooping in humiliation, wounded in body and pride. But we petted him better – he had done his best and anyway it had been a very close thing.

Of the prince of the forest, the bushbuck, we saw very little. If one saw us before we saw it, we hardly saw it at all. Often they must have passed from sight without us ever being aware of their presence. Their passage over the forest floor's leaf-mould mattress was utterly soundless and their dark pelage, patterned with white disruptive spots, merged and disappeared in the enveloping gloom.

We angled in cool quiet streams with bamboo rods and bent pins in water so clear we could watch the fish rising. For bait we dug fat wriggling earthworms from the rich humus all around and broiled our catch of small redfin tilapia that, secured through our own enterprise, tasted far superior to ordinary home-cooking. When the rains came and the streams churned with brown torrential water we hauled in writhing dappled eels, swept down by the current from deep pools upstream in the heart of the forest – parts we had never explored.

We were careful not to venture too far from familiar paths as it was said that Zulu witchdoctors used the seclusion of the inner forest to practise ritual murders and that certain anatomical bits and pieces of white boys were highly prized medicine. We were told this by our parents and if we questioned their word it was reinforced by friends – co-conspirators – whose experience and sagacity was beyond repute. The idea was to discourage us from wandering too far afield. They also mentioned the existence of a leopard that no one had ever seen but was reckoned to be highly dangerous. It alone, they said, had survived after the

others had been shot and in its lonely vengeful state of mind held humans in very low regard.

I was fascinated by the thought of the leopard sharing the forest with me, perhaps watching from cover without revealing itself. Whenever I visited Dlinza I searched the ground for its mark without any success. I half hoped for and half dreaded a meeting – would it sense that I presented no threat, that I was an ally?

Most of all I needed to believe in its existence and so, in the end, I think, did most of the adults, for in repeating the legend to their children, the ogre of their cautionary tale assumed substance and they came to believe in it as much as we did. Today when I tease my mother about the mythical leopard she looks at me in surprise and denies it was a fabrication. Nobody ever saw it of course, but yes, it was there.

More tangible were the bush pigs – nocturnal visitors to our vegetable patch. They came straight through the barbwire surrounding the property to root amongst the potatoes and carrots. In the morning I would find tufts of bristle caught in the barbs and thrill as I rolled the wiry hair between my fingertips, imagining them as they must have looked – primitive and dangerous.

As a family we threatened the pigs with dire consequences if we ever caught them at their trespasses, but like the vervet monkeys that ripped up our pea plants and carried off near-ripe pawpaws or the mongoose that raided the chicken run after fresh-laid eggs, my brother and I would have been heartbroken had they ceased to return. More

Creatures of the forest: High above the forest floor a leopard guards the remains of its bushbuck kill; a shy, mostly nocturnal blue duiker ram – the secretions from his prominent facial glands are used to mark territory; a vervet monkey suckles her infant; left, the prince of the forest, an elegant bushbuck ram.

than anything else, more than our recent introduction to the secrets of reading and writing, we valued our contacts with the natural world our perimeter fence sought to exclude.

Night drives back from visits to neighbours were voyages into a new dimension as nightjars and owls ghosted up from the gravel road; hares, trapped in the headlights' beam, zigzagged ahead seeking escape and once or twice a bushbuck, momentarily transfixed, eyes aglow, turned to slip back into the darkness.

All this I took for granted as I did the Zulus who lived and laboured alongside us. The bare-breasted, bare-footed women went about their business as they had always done and the men, with easy smiles and stretched earlobes, never deigning to learn any language other than their own, worked when they needed to. Boys my own age taught me to skin and cure the miniature, glossy pelts of moles we trapped in the garden and the art of dropping edible birds with a slingshot. We herded cattle together in fields of grass that stood above our heads and learnt which wild fruits could be eaten and which were poisonous.

Days turned from hot summer sunshine to crisp frosty winter nights around a log fire in a languorous cycle. Then, after four years, it suddenly ended. The business failed and we moved to a city. Only then did I appreciate how much I had had and how much I had lost.

Now, after 25 years, I was returning – this time with Margot. In the interim I had lived in other parts of Africa, in Europe and Australia. I went back to Zululand for no better reason than to be there. I was drawn by its wildlife and its people and the spiritual sanctuary I had once known. Not that I imagined I could recapture the original magic – that special brand of innocence and enchantment is reserved for childhood – but it seemed worthwhile, indeed essential, amidst the rush of change carrying us down unfriendly corridors of confrontation and alienation, to recognize and attempt to define what has and is being lost and what might yet be saved.

As a result of the carving up and redistribution of land that has taken place the term 'Zululand' as a geographical entity, has little meaning today. There still ex-

ists, however, a popular concept of what constitutes Zululand and for practical reasons I have retained those boundaries. They are much the same as those defended by Cetshwayo at the time of Lord Chelmsford's campaign against the Zulu nation in 1879.

Zululand begins in the east where the Indian Ocean breaks against hard white beaches. Towering forested dunes, in places over 150 metres high and thought to be the tallest in the world, run parallel to the coastline from Zululand's southern limit at the Tugela River mouth to its northern point, Kosi Bay, on the Moçambique border. Behind the dunes where the land levels out is a chain of freshwater lakes and papyrus swamps fed by seasonal streams which often have no direct outlet to the sea.

The interior rises in a series of terraces from the comparatively flat coastal forest plains westwards to where the present-day Hluhluwe and Umfolozi game reserves occupy the foothills of the first escarpment rising from the plains. Here the productive bushveld of sweet savannas and thorn-tree woodlands predominates, overflowing with mammals, birds and insects, smells, colours and sounds. It was an earthly paradise, exulted by Nathaniel Isaacs, one of the first 'swallows' – an early Zulu name for Whites who, like these birds, built their homes from adobe – to visit the country: 'On the summit of the mountain we had a most commanding view of the interior, which here exhibited considerable verdure, the scenery on each side of us being rich beyond description. I cannot

The forest's muted pristine spaces, far left, are illuminated by vivid bracket fungi. Devoid of chlorophyll, fungi cannot manufacture their own food as can green plants. Some, called saprophytes, derive nourishment from the dead bark of trees or other dead organic material, centre. A Knysna loerie flares for a brief fire-coloured moment under the high forest's canopy. A tree frog, silent and unmoving, uses the sucker-like discs on its toes and fingers to anchor itself to the smooth surface of its perch.

A long-tailed widow trails his breeding plumage in slow deliberate flight. In the old days Zulu warriors used the widow's extravagant tail feathers to decorate their headdresses.

fancy a more charming spot; I think I scarcely ever saw one exceeding it; it really looked like a fairy land, with Arcadian beauties on every side: the scattered huts of the natives – the cattle indulging in the rich pasturage – cultivated patches rising ever and anon on the inequalities of the surface – the adjacent hills towering one above the other in all the magnificence of picturesque form – presented such a combination of objects that we were almost perplexed in admiration of their variety. Here we halted and refreshed ourselves, contemplating the beauties of nature scattered over the extended scene.'

On the high, bracing central plateau – the roof of Zululand – rolling montane grasslands lapped temperate mist forests which must have once seemed as deep and indestructible as the sea.

Up to 10 000 years ago the eastern side of Africa was covered with rain forests until a drier climatic cycle greatly reduced their extent. Many life forms adapted to the new order but others, unable to do so, passed into extinction. Within the closed depths of the remaining forests, however, life continued much as before. Here, live creatures that over the millennia have had little need to adapt to changing circumstances have, of consequence, remained conservative in appearance and behaviour.

Zululand's marvellously varied landmass is intersected throughout by river torrents that course down steep valleys, then trickle oily slow across the bottomlands, their progress traced by narrow fingers of riparian jungle. Occasionally the topography's even tenor is startlingly

disrupted, as by the brooding Lebombo mountains dramatically flung up above the Tongaland coastal plains during a period of intense geological change that reshaped Africa.

All this I wished to savour, knowing full well that much of it had already changed. I would have to content myself with what had been preserved – the 'witness areas' that, protected by law, bear testimony to what had once been.

Yet enough remained to fire me with a rush of enthusiasm and anticipation for what lay ahead and I hurried to complete our preparations. After arranging the itinerary and supplies my chief concern was securing permission from the various conservation authorities and governmental bodies to allow us the freedom to investigate all and everything as much as we pleased. This necessitated flying trips

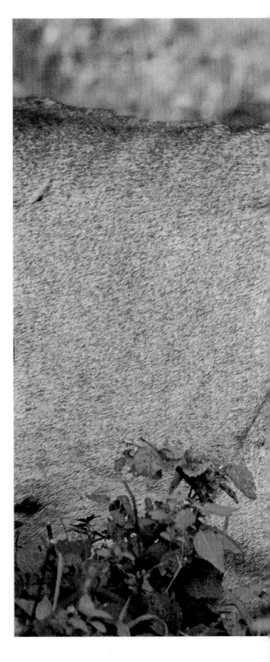

to Pietermaritzburg, Natal's sleepy provincial capital and Ulundi, KwaZulu's newly constituted seat of government, to enlist the help and co-operation of the Natal Parks Board and the KwaZulu Nature Conservation Division. Then to Pretoria, for permits to enter restricted tribal homelands.

I based myself in Johannesburg during this time as it was central and able to furnish, at best possible price, all my requirements. As soon as my preparatory chores were complete I quit its glitzy mean-spirited environs with a profound sense of relief.

In the chill of a hazy dawn I drove through bleery suburbs, passed bus-shelters full of working women, all smoking, faces set in lines of permanent discontent, leaning into their early morning cigarettes with fierce unfocused avidity. Buses jammed with black commuters lurched and belched, the crumpled expressions of anonymous passengers disembodied behind smudged windowpanes, proclaimed only the fatigue of living. Altogether a good place to be leaving and I was on my way.

The broad, smooth highway swept across the pastoral uplands of the Transvaal, past endless rows of maturing maize. Spherical silos waiting to receive the crop stood stark against a treeless horizon. The only breaks in the monotony were the wattle and daub homesteads of Ndebele farm labourers that periodically hove into sight. The Ndebele decorate the exterior walls of their shacks with colourful, bold designs and images from everyday life. These depictions – a group of stick figures waving or pointing to an aeroplane flying overhead and a dog (or

In the Hluhluwe-Umfolozi complex where Zululand's only wild lion population occurs, a bloody faced lioness gnaws on her meagre share of an impala fawn that moments before had been torn apart by competing pride members. Lions stand at the top of the terrestrial food chain as they have done in these parts for nearly five million years.

is it a horse) off to one side ignoring the fuss – are set down with vivid childlike strokes. This harmonious fusion of traditional crafts and modern influences allowed me a glimpse into episodes from the lives of these peasant artists as well as an opportunity to interpret the vital illustrations as best I could.

My first destination was Hluhluwe Game Reserve, a famous sanctuary with which I was familiar and where I have always experienced a pervasive peace of mind. It has never failed me. It casts a spell that defies articulation, weaving a physical and spiritual sense of wellbeing that stimulates as it relaxes.

Hluhluwe takes its name from a thorny creeper, *Dalbergia armata* – umhluhluwe in Zulu – that grows throughout the bushveld and forests and along riverbanks. The Zulus use its slender ropy branches as muzzles for their calves to prevent them suckling and, like so much else within Hluhluwe's restricted spaces, it grows everywhere in profusion.

I selected Hluhluwe as a starting point both as a personal indulgence to cleanse the aftertaste of too many weeks of city living, and to establish a mood, create a yardstick, by which to measure the state of affairs prevailing throughout the rest of rural Zululand. It was in many ways a measure of the successes, failures, aspirations and problems current in the territory's wildlife estate.

Together with Umfolozi and St Lucia, Hluhluwe is the oldest proclaimed game reserve in Africa. It was legislated into existence in April 1897 – a year before Kruger Park – by a Zululand government finally roused to action by furious public protests arising from news reports that a hunting party had, in 1894, shot six white rhinoceros, a species already so rare as to be thought extinct by many.

Almost from its inception Hluhluwe was buffeted by the traumas of a controversy still raging today, which supposedly sets the best interests of people against those of wildlife. Human needs, it is argued, must come before those of wild animals – though in the long view the distinction is a false one, for in the eclipse of nature lies our own demise.

Wracked by the insensate slaughter of big game during the anti-tsetse fly campaigns of the 1920s and 1940s, poaching and demands for its deproclamation by

land-hungry farmers, Hluhluwe survived although its trials are not by any means over.

Like most other parks in Zululand, Hluhluwe has what are termed 'sharp-edged' borders that abut densely populated tribal lands without the cushioning effect of less populated 'buffer zones'. The boundary fences that keep animals in and people out also demarcate the troubled first line of defence separating isolated pockets of wild country from increasingly overcrowded rural homelands. In satellite photographs Zululand's parks show up like oases in an ecological desert.

Chief Minister of KwaZulu, Gatsha Buthelezi has warned: 'Contrary to the expectations of many, I am a wilderness enthusiast . . . but my people are land-hungry. This faces them more and more with the issue of survival within the reality of their situation. This means that more and more of my people, who with me belong to the wilderness of Africa, see my enthusiasm for the wilderness getting less and less relevant to the major issue of just their sheer survival.'

His observation has great significance, for in the past parks had limited objectives and served a very small segment of the population. For their future survival however, these objectives have to be relevant to the population as a whole and now that time and space have run out we are down to our last options. With this in mind I wanted to immerse myself in the endangered places, to understand fully what we still hold in trust and what we risk losing.

Hluhluwe is only about 23 000 hectares in extent although it is connected by the corridor to Umfolozi, a contiguous area of 96 000 hectares with no manmade or, with the silting of major rivers, any real natural barriers separating these two parks. The whole is referred to simply as the Complex and later I went south to Umfolozi for an extended stay.

For my first outing I arranged a conducted reconnaissance off the regular tourist roads, not in anticipation of seeing more game but purely for greater seclusion. I started early to avoid the oppressive mid-day heat, plunging down rutted tracks flanked by dense *Euclea* thickets with visibility very limited. Not until breaking through into more open

An old giraffe bull stares down with mild reproach then unexpectedly whips out a long pink tongue and nonchalantly wipes his nose.

Wild dogs playfully wrestle in prelude to a hunt. These consummate hunters were once common in Zululand but disappeared from the Hluhluwe-Umfolozi complex in the late 1920s. A small number have recently been re-introduced to Hluhluwe.

woodland did I begin to encounter wildlife in any numbers. A small herd of buffalo went rocking away, their attendant oxpeckers hurrying to keep up. A black rhino cow with an accompanying subadult calf wheeled in confusion at the racket of our sudden approach. Horn lofted in the air she peered dimly about, trying to make up her rudimentary mind whether or not to charge, then the two of them turned, kicking up dust in precipitant retreat. A flock of crowned guineafowl scuttled panic-stricken ahead of the Landrover, explosively starting up at the last moment to flutter and glide out of harm's way. A dark old giraffe bull stared down at the commotion with a look of mild reproach then unexpectedly whipped out a long pink tongue and nonchalantly wiped his nose.

Impala and nyala are particularly numerous here although in the 1930s both species were so scarce as to warrant reintroductions from Mkuzi. Since then there has been a staggering increase to the extent that they now top the culling 'hit' list. Their population explosion is in response to the increase in suitable habitat as creeping bush encroachment invades open grasslands now degraded through overuse. Bush encroachment has always been a major ecological problem in Hluhluwe and control methods involving mechanical equipment, chemicals and fire have all been tried and found in the long term to be ineffectual.

A species' density in any given area is in direct proportion to the suitability of the locality to its special requirements. When an ecological upheaval such as bush encroachment occurs it tips the balance in favour of bush-loving animals like impala and nyala and against those such as waterbuck and reedbuck that rely on grasslands for food and cover and whose populations in Hluhluwe have crashed in consequence. Predation does not limit the prey species' natural increase in a stable ecosystem, rather the reverse is true; the availability of herbivores controls carnivore numbers.

Predators are well represented in Hluhluwe and the recent re-introduction of wild dogs means that with the exception of brown hyenas, its former large predator diversity has been restored. There is still however a question mark over the future of the wild dogs. The

animals themselves are doing well, hunting and breeding successfully, but their instinctive wanderlust is getting them into trouble. They crawl under the gameproof boundary fence where it crosses dry riverbeds and though they return, pressure might be applied to take action against them if complaints are received concerning stock losses whenever they stray.

Wild dogs were once common in Zululand. The last definite record in the Complex, however, was as far back as 1928 after which all evidence points to some unknown epidemic eliminating those survivors of an anti-vermin campaign. Old Mkuzi residents remember wild dogs as being fairly common during the 1930s but last sighting was around 1948. The return of a small number to their former range will have no appreciable ecological impact but would be of tremendous aesthetic appeal.

Lions have recolonized Hluhluwe as young animals evicted from Umfolozi's breeding nucleus have wandered north, and the highlight of our trip was the discovery of a pride of 11 feeding off the carcass of a buffalo bull they must have cornered, then killed in the Hluhluwe River. Only the buffalo's head and withers were above the surface and the single adult male stood chestdeep in water, using his knife-edged molars to slice into the rump while the rest of the pride crouched flank to flank on the riverbank, gnawing at the thick hide.

Lions evoke a primal fascination and I considered this sighting, so soon and under such dramatic circumstances, to be a good omen. I approached not so close as to disturb them but close enough to hear clearly the moist sucking sound of rending flesh and the low guttural growls exchanged between competing pride members. Barbel churned the water in pursuit of scraps and vultures, like huge galls on the bare branches of a dead tree, waited their chance. All of creation's dynamic life-forces seemed to flow from that Pleistocene tableau of sky, water and trees, feeding lions and patient birds; the conversion of life into death into energy and so back into life, reduced to its seminal components. It was easy to imagine that little had changed from the time in November 1856 when one of the early white hunters to visit Zululand, William Baldwin, recorded in his diary: 'Crossed the St Luey (Hluhluwe), one of the best rivers I know of for sports of all kinds, and nearest to the Colony (Natal); it rises somewhere at the foot of the Ombombo (Lebombo) Mountains and runs through a splendid wooded valley. Lions are very plentiful.'

On the way home a group of zebra broke off grazing as I drew alongside and in profile one revealed a deeply impressed scar circling its neck, left by a wirenoose snare. This animal escaped but many do not and while poaching has been around as long as there have been conservation laws, it has of late assumed ominous proportions. Where in the past poaching meant providing only enough meat to fill a few cooking pots, the situation was not too serious, but often these days food is no longer the motivation. Over the last two decades in East and Central Africa the problem has been compounded by the ease with which modern weapons can be obtained, corruption in high places and the spiralling prices of ivory and rhino horn. Added to a drastic reduction in the standard of living, this combination of factors has sparked off an unprecedented poaching epidemic that is unlikely to abate in the near future and will probably get worse.

Zululand has no grounds for complacency where poaching is concerned. Hunting and snaring is a major problem on tribal lands and not long ago the Natal Parks Board was shocked when one of their own gamescouts was apprehended after shooting two rhino for their horns and a buffalo for its meat.

I spent a further four days re-acquainting myself with Hluhluwe. It is beautiful country; an harmonious blend of ancient plains encircled by high bald hills, their wooded slopes giving way to grassy crests. In the northern highlands moist semi-deciduous gallery forests occur above the 300-metre contour where rare primordial relics benefit from a higher annual rainfall than areas below that altitude. Blue duiker and shy arboreal samango monkeys thrive in these forests.

On early mornings I watched herds of black African buffalo, with low-slung horns and distrustful mien, emerge from the Mpanzakazi thickets to be met by their attendant cattle egrets and make their way down to the good grazing of the Manzibomvu Valley. I once saw a leopard flushed from the forest canopy come down through the branches with the agility of a night-ape, stand momentarily poised on a supporting branch, gloriously illuminated by a shaft of undiluted immortal light, before springing from sight into the impenetrable shadows where it lived.

On this latest visit I found myself particularly attracted to these climax forests, their darkly silent trees in such dramatic counterpoint to the vast, barren, remorseless Skeleton Coast of the Namib Desert where I had last worked.

Nothing could be more different than the throbbing greenness of this circumscribed vegetal world I had entered. Life swarmed all around and the cool stillness of the forest creaked with the feeling of movement, of secret stirrings, the close rustle of leaves – sounds at the edge of silence – a white tambourine dove in a cabbage tree, then a fire-coloured moment in the high canopy as a purple-crested loerie flared into flight. Buffalo dung on the trail, so fresh it seemed to breathe and a warm brown lingering

buffalo smell. I quickly paused to assess the situation and the quiet was shattered by the demented shrieking of a trumpeter hornbill. In the stunned silence that followed my heart hammered wildly. An unconcerned butterfly trailing light from its gaudy wings flitted from out of the gloom to dance above the flat steaming pats. From ahead came a shifting of shadow and light, the fleeting presence of some wild creature sensed rather than seen, incorporeal as the leopard of my childhood.

The steep path levelled out on reaching a lateral ridge where shallow leached soils inhibit the growth of trees and the forest, its edges sharply defined by past fires, giving way to grasslands. The sudden emergence from forest confines into this sun-splashed airy upland was like surfacing after a deep dive. Vision was abruptly telescoped to reveal a wide wild lovely lonely panorama of earth and sky; an immense vibrant tapestry, unequivocally African.

It is a timeless prospect, immeasurably old. Older than mankind, as old as the hills where I stood surrounded by sun and wind and circling crows. On the Nzimane flats below were wildebeest etched darkly against new grass, their patient grazing emphasizing the immutability and perfection of basic rhythms. Time had no weight – it passed slowly, while all the land waited and listened.

A knot of kudu, brownish-grey with faint white vertical stripes like quartz veins in granite, took note of my arrival, stared for one long hard moment, then bounded away. Beneath a spreading acacia a lone rhino lay in an angular heap and in the middle distance was the Nzimane River, winding silver through dark thorn forest. These hills and valleys, forests and savannas seem to stretch to the horizon and on – bursting with life. Yet much of what I saw was a deception. Across the river where distance erases detail, the country is occupied by tribesmen and has, for the most part, been used up. Weeds have replaced grass and mature trees have been felled for firewood. Where I stood is not far from Hluhluwe's western boundary but beyond that everything changes.

The following day I left Hluhluwe on my way to KwaZulu, to see for myself. The first leg of the journey was uneventful until towards noon when I departed the highway and shortly thereafter saw the last of the neatly-ordered, White-owned farms. The road wound down off the escarpment, dipping and rising through dells and razorback ridges, passed Makabeleni, Jameson's Drift, Klolwana, Qudeni, the gravel surface steadily deteriorating the deeper I drove into KwaZulu.

As the rural homeland of the Zulus is undeveloped, KwaZulu's chief industry is of necessity the raising of crops and livestock, but contrary to the mental picture one has of a farming community, my first and most lasting impression on entering was of people, everywhere filling the land. Children alongside the road returned my waves with wide-open smiles, while their older siblings, closer to the cutting edge of survival and less friendly, resorted to begging or touting crude tourist gimcracks, then raised quick fists when their blandishments went unanswered. Young women consorted in coveys, bright sprigs of bougainvillea set in their berets and sexually segregated groups of adults in disintegrating city clothes broke off conferring to watch us pass, right arms raised in grave salute.

Whenever I stopped I invited a mobbing. People gathered immediately, crowding round with strident voices and waving arms; some to solicit handouts, others offering anything from wood carvings to shards of quartz for sale. A minority seemed drawn by nothing more than curiosity and a few furtive ones prowled round the car in the ill-concealed hope of pilfering if the chance presented.

They came in the expectation that I might have something to offer and because they had nothing else to do. Like refugees adrift in a war-zone of grinding poverty, impelled by the desperation of their situation, they seized at every opportunity. Yet remarkably, in spite of the deprivation and stress of living so close to the famine line, their natural ebullience bubbled through. Once a few purchases had been made and the small change distributed amongst the youngsters, they obligingly formed up, giggling self-consciously, to have their picture taken, then saw me off with whoops of 'Hamba Kahle!' (go well!), running alongside until the vehicle outstripped

When an ecological upheaval such as bush encroachment occurs in game parks it tips the balance in favour of bush-loving animals like impala and nyala and against those such as waterbuck and reedbuck that rely on grasslands for food and cover.

A beautiful scourge, opposite page – the Chinese lantern bush (Dichrostachys cinerea) – invades impoverished, overgrazed lands where it tends to form impenetrable thickets.

The zebra's woodland habitat is also hardpressed. KwaZulu's burgeoning human population must now farm the background hills where already annual grasses have replaced perennials and mature trees are felled for firewood; the red earth showing through is a precursor to more serious damage, such as gully erosion, page 28.

The destruction of habitat through such crude farming practices as 'slash-and-burn', right, leads to deforestation, overgrazing and acceleration of soil erosion – the whole dismal cycle that accompanies human overcrowding.

Simple pleasures are enjoyed by youngsters the world over, and KwaZulu children are no exception. However, daily tasks such as gathering woodfire and carrying water are begun early in life. All generations come together at the local store, not always meeting approval.

them. As I pulled away I wondered how much longer this good-natured stoicism could endure.

KwaZulu is in serious trouble. It is the most densely populated rural area in South Africa with a human population that will double in 20 years. The explosively expanding population is destroying finite resources, pushing KwaZulu towards a state of ecological collapse. The destruction of habitat through poor farming practices, deforestation, overgrazing and accelerating soil erosion – the whole dismal cycle that accompanies overcrowding – has locked the land into a downward spiral of degradation.

As Professor John Hanks, Director of the Institute of Natural Resources pointed out: 'Cultivation of hilly areas, with their fragile soil, plus too many people and too much stock in too small an area are the main contributors to the appalling erosion apparent in many parts of the province. Millions of tons of soil are washed annually into the sea.'

Added to the erosion problem is what has been termed 'the poor man's fuel crisis', with the hills and valleys of Kwa-Zulu being stripped of their trees by people in need of firewood for cooking and heating. Firewood is already scarce, brought in by tribeswomen who have walked many kilometres to collect the meagre faggots on their heads. Research has shown that wood consumption in KwaZulu is just under one ton per person per year. At that rate the growth in the human population is outpacing the growth of new trees and the catastrophic acceleration of deforestation results in yet more soil erosion and severe flooding. Once all the firewood is gone, country folk resort to burning cakes of dried livestock dung to cook their food, thus depriving the soil of precious manure that would nourish it.

Yet it is no good telling local populations, who are obliged to cut down trees in order to get domestic fuel or pasture for livestock or land for cultivation, that they can no longer do so, unless an immediate alternative is provided.

It was not always this way. A hundred years ago the trader-chronicler David Leslie noted that 'the Zulu country must be very thinly populated, for the extent; as, from the hill, I saw at least fifty miles on either side, and on the seaward at least seventy and, within my view there was no more than thirty kraals. Mr Schraeder (the missionary) said the population of the Zulu country is over 200 000 . . .' Today there are ten times as many people occupying the same amount of land.

Before the advent of the white man the Zulu population remained essentially constant. As a natural expedient a high birthrate was inherent to Zulu culture to offset the vicissitudes of primitive life. Attrition in the form of internecine warfare, disease and drought ensured that there was enough land to spare for the survivors and their cattle, creating a balance as perpetuating as that governing the wildlife with which they co-existed.

The Zulu tribal system established a way of life that was timeless and unchanging. Change, in fact, was actively discouraged as a threat to the even tenor of society. Then almost overnight it was dramatically torn asunder. In the contest of wills pitting the world's foremost colonial power against Africa's last great Iron Age army, any conclusion other than that which ultimately prevailed was inconceivable. The punished impis withdrew. A new power had replaced them in Zululand and its imperial emissaries were soon busy adjudicating and evangelizing. War, summary execution and cattle raiding was outlawed. By and large the subjugated Zulus conformed to the new restrictions and continued breeding as before – that custom still being legal.

The balance between the forces of life and death gradually tilted in favour of life. Populations began to expand and before long the rising tide of consumers threatened to outpace the natural productiveness of the land. The genius of science combatted diseases until human life itself became a disease on the overworked land. In the old physically comfortable years only a fraction as many relied on the same resources, having bought their material blessings at the price of a high mortality rate. With the safeguards removed natural systems staggered under the burden, faltered, then slipped into the present perilous spiral.

KwaZulu is still inextricably linked to agriculture, yet generally its agricultural performance is poor, a consequence of inadequate training and illiteracy.

As a result of low expectations and income from a rapidly deteriorating subsistence economy a rural drain is in progress as the more ambitious young men turn to the cities seeking work opportunities, and tragically leaving agriculture in the hands of the elderly and least able.

Unless solutions are found and implemented Zululand will face its most cataclysmic era with none of the bold calls to arms of Chaka's legions or Her Majesty's Redcoats, but with the ringing silence of privation and starvation. Professor Hanks argues that 'positive strategies for the survival of these degraded areas and the people who live there, are not as remote as many would have us believe. What KwaZulu urgently requires is a positive rural landuse strategy which recognizes the prime importance of food production, but at the same time safeguards soil and representative areas of natural ecosystems.'

Damage to the land is not always apparent. Often you have to know what to look for. Canyons of surrealistically sculptured earth caused by gully erosion were plain to see but in this corner of KwaZulu early rains had brought forth a mantle of young grass that disguised the scars. The hills rolled gently away, tranquil and enduring, radiating a quality that quietened the mind.

Nearby a clapper lark enthusiastically celebrated the return of the breeding season. Singing was not enough; he flung himself into the air out of sheer romantic exuberance, his wingbeats producing a series of sharp claps that crackled and reverberated in the absence of all other sound. Insect-harvesting swallows tossed on the high wind like dark blown leaves while closer to earth a skein of white egrets flopped across bulky clouds black with rain.

For once the country was empty of people except for a lonely figure standing on a hillcrest, mute and fixed against the horizon. He stared wild-eyed as I hurried past, his tatters blowing in the wind like the last surviving witness to the apocalypse.

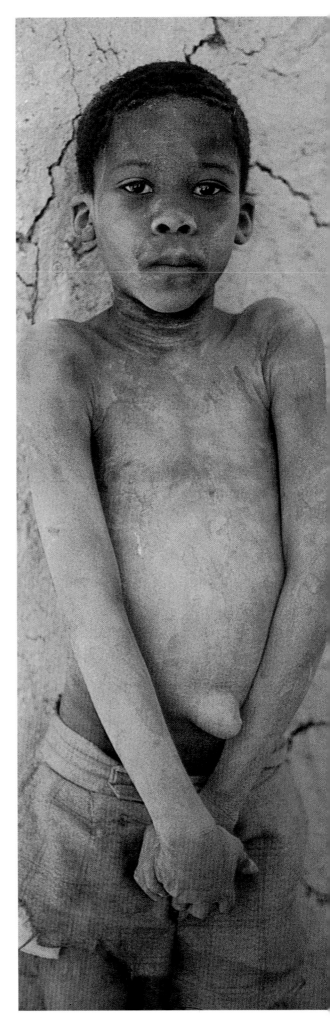

Unless solutions are found to Zululand's serious land erosion none of the bold calls to arms of Chaka's legions will stave off the reality of abject poverty and starvation.

A ZULU ROMANCE

'Thou hast finished off the tribes
Where will thou wage war?
Yes! where wilt thou wage war?
Thou has conquered the kings
Yes! Yes! Yes!
Where wilt thou wage war?'

Recited by his subjects in praise of
Chaka King of the Zulus 1804 – 1828

Their clan name was as sublime as a benediction – abakwaZulu, the people of Heaven. For 300 years from their founding by Zulu, son of Malandela until Chaka's chieftaincy in 1804 they enjoyed a tranquil agrarian existence a few kilometres south of the White Umfolozi River. On these fertile wild pastures they grazed their valuable herds of cattle and constructed comfortable villages of hive-shaped huts. Their cohesive perpetuating way of life was stabilized and reinforced by a pervasive ethic of social and religious tradition. They and their neighbours lived much as their common ancestors had during the thousands of years the drifting southward migration took to bring them from Nyanzaland (Central Africa) to their present destination. The Zulus were an undistinguished Nguni clan among many. One man's genius was to change all that.

The Zulu empire was forged on the anvil of Chaka's ambition and fuelled by his vengeful anger stemming from childhood taunts regarding his illegitimate birth. The embittered boy developed into a physical and mental giant with a breadth of concept and single-mindedness unprecedented in contemporary black African affairs. Unlike the inconclusive posturing that till then had passed as battles, Chaka waged war in the grand manner – remorseless and total. From chief of a tiny Zulu principality of 1 500 people, he expanded his powerbase through conquest and assimilation until his assassination 12 years later at the age of 41, by which time he controlled two million subjects, maintained a superbly disciplined army of 50 000 warriors and ruled an area ten times greater than present day Zululand (of which his original inheritance constituted only one percent), while his 'shadow' hovered over territory 12 times greater still.

So formidable was this monolithic African state that it survived mismanagement by Chaka's inept successors, Dingane and Mpande, and under King Cetshwayo rose up in 1879, 63 years from its inception, and engaged a British force of 20 000 infantry and cavalry bearing breech-loading rifles, cannon and rockets, who were supported by Colonial mounted troops and thousands of Natal Native levies, many of them armed with rifles. In a campaign that lasted six months the Zulu nation was eventually crushed but not before inflicting in the battle of Isandlwana the most grievous military defeat ever suffered by modern soldiers at the hands of 'savages'.

Britain had embarked on the war intent on destroying the independent Zulu nation-state, thus removing the perceived threat it posed to the neighbouring Natal colony. In the aftermath Zululand found itself without an army or a king – Cetshwayo having been captured and exiled to Cape Town – and under the authority of the Crown. The new conquerors were determined to dismantle the House of Chaka and ensure that it could not be resurrected. The old order was thus doomed and Zululand had no choice but to come to terms with the new.

Zulu domestic life had always been a model of manners, discipline and social virtues. The dominant rule was obedience – by children to their parents, villagers to their chief and by everyone to the king. The intrusion of alien European laws and customs rocked the conservative tribal system but where possible change continued to be resisted. More recently however many Zulus have become urbanized and the challenge this has presented to traditional cultural and moral values has frequently resulted in great psychological and social problems. Zulus who have most successfully adjusted to irreverent modernity have done so by retaining some of the tradition while keeping alive the memory of their proud history.

While researching old publications in the Africana archives I came across a volume printed in 1875 for a private collection entitled 'Among the Zulus and Amatongas' by David Leslie and edited by W H Drummond, one of Zululand's most renowned early white hunters. In it Leslie records a campfire tale told him by an old warrior which vividly brings to life the spirit and attitudes that prevailed in Zululand before their army's final defeat at the Battle of Ulundi. It recounts a highlight in an old man's life and although not representative of day to day living it does provide a fascinating insight into an era that has so glibly been dismissed by some as 'nasty, brutish and short'. On the contrary, an old soldier

speaks of an age that is stirring, fruitful and sorely missed. This is his story:

'What is it we like most of all? We like war! Is there anything that equals it? No! no! certainly not. We fight nowhere now. You white men have encircled us; but perhaps the day may come when you will allow us to pass through your country, and remind those nobody's people that the Zulus are still on the face of the earth. We would not meddle with your cattle. We hear that the outside tribes say we sway no-one now but the Amatonga (looked upon as women and dogs). When will you let us prove that we can do more? It may be, as you say, that fighting is wrong, but we have not yet learnt to think so. It is true that the country is quieter and that all live in comparative safety, but what of that? There are none of us now that can say they are braves. We might as well be

Isandlwana Hill, where, in 1879, the Zulu army under King Cetshwayo inflicted a grievous military defeat on Lord Chelmsford's 'red soldiers'.

A Swazi herdsman musters Nguni cattle, a traditional breed, practically non-existent today, characterized by their small size and symmetrical markings – those on one flank mirror those on the other. Their size was of great importance when the Swazis hid them in mountain caves during Zulu raids.

* Zulus believed that the spirits of their fathers watched over them and that these spirits resided in snakes. The spirits of chiefs reside in a boomslang, of kings in a mamba and common people turn into a number of different species. These snakes are distinguished from the rest as being 'spirit snakes'. Other ordinary kinds are dismissed as mere reptiles.

women. Yes, many people were killed in the old – men, women and children – but that was nothing; it kept us from crowding. The cows had more room to get fat, and we to make our gardens. And then, besides, the young men had a chance of getting cattle, and, when they sewed the ring on their heads, wives. Now, we are poor all our days. Then, we had people amongst us who had a name through the country for valour and for cunning; now, no one is known except the chiefs and the King. Then, we had something to live and die for, some excitement in our lives; now, all the soldiers are good for is to build or mend the King's kraals, or hoe his corn. We all see what it is coming to; we shall all pay money to you white men at last (taxes), and take to digging down hills under you (roadmaking etc). Ah! the army, my man, the army! There's something to talk about when that goes. You want me to tell you of some exploits in which I shared; well,

wait till I take some snuff and then I'll do it. Make up the fire, boy.

Long ago in the aforetime – how many years, say you? How should I know? two hundred may be; yes, so many (showing two fingers); I was a young man, and strong. Hau! but I was strong and active. I could throw every man in our regiment. When I ran, people used to exclaim, 'Hau! just now he was here, and now he is yonder; where did he go?' And when I jumped I went till I struck the sky. Is it hard, say you? Don't, white man, don't; you are laughing at me now. Let me tell my story my own way. You understand our tongue and ways. Here, my equal, help me in the nose (asking another for snuff). Eh-h-h! man of our tribe (thanking him). As I was saying, long, long ago it was once decided by the King and chiefs to make a raid into the amaSwazi – a King's raid. I mean that the King was getting short of cattle; and as it was known that the amaSwazi had

again gathered herds since the last war, we were to be sent to bring him some. It was denied to anyone to take what he could manage to get away out of the herd, as you know this is always allowed in other wars. Well, well, it is not exactly allowed; but nothing is said if the man can get clear off. This time, however, it was announced that spies would be sent all over the country, and anyone found with cattle he could not account for, would be killed. They also told us that all girls we took should be brought to the King, to form his slaves of the interior. As I have said, we are fond enough of war, but we like to look forward to some reward at the end; so to us young men these orders were peculiarly unpalatable; we loathed, and many were the talks we had in discussing, this expedition. I decided, for my part, that there was no harm done. I should of course go out, and be guided by circumstances. If my snake* was favourable, I should not re-

33

Elaborate headdresses denote the married status of these Zulu women.

turn empty-handed, for all the orders. If not, and I showed above the others, the King might perhaps soften, and give me something. Anyway, I had to go.

All Zulu was gathered together at Nodwengo (the King's kraal). By twos and threes, tens and two tens, they came trooping over the hills. Others, whose headquarters were further off, came in their regiments. The earth thundered with the noise of their feet. Our ears were closed up with the sound of their songs. The country all around was black with their forms by day, and was red with the fires they lit at night. The clatter of sticks and shields was continually heard, as they hustled together in the joyous excitement of fight.

It was the beginning of the war; and no cattle could graze where the army had been, till after the next rains. Ah-h-h, the Zulu, my man; Zulu!! can they be spoken of? (in a manner competent to describe them).

Well, one day we hungered, and another day we feasted, just as the King happened to give us beer and beef. At last our number was complete, the generals appointed, and we started on our way. As we went, the people hid their food and fled with their cattle, into almost inaccessible places. Nevertheless, we managed to get at them and fed. Our path was known by the cattle bones which strewed it, by the remains of dishes and corn, and here and there a body. Whose people were they, say you? Why, our own – the Zulus. The assegai had got loose, my man, and who was to stop it? We walked long. We hungered. We crossed many rivers, but we never tired. We began to long for some opposition, just to vary the monotony, but none was to be seen. You must know that the 'Swazi country is full of large caves, the secret of the entrances to which is rigidly kept. They are so large that all the people of a district, together with their cattle, can take shelter in them: and they had done so on the report of our coming. We were travelling along a ridge of mountains, when the sound of cattle lowing was heard, seemingly underneath and all about us. A halt

was called, to consider how we should get at them. Parties were sent out in all directions to try and fall on an opening, but, for a long time, none could they find. At last one of them came upon a small hole in the rock, of size about sufficient for a man to creep in. One was instantly directed to make the attempt, and laying down his shield, he took an assegai in one hand, and in he went. We heard a shout, a groan, and all was still; our man came not back. Another was at once sent after him, and shared the same fate. Now we began to hang back. It was certain death to refuse; it seemed to be the same to go in. So far it was equal; but we loathed the idea of being killed like a porcupine in a hole. I considered for a moment, and then it struck me that I had the idea, and I said to myself, 'Now is the time to show above the others; now for some cattle.' I spoke out; I cried out, 'I will go in.' 'Who is that?' inquired one of the officers.

'Myself, father,' I answered.

'Appear!' was the next word, and I did so. I was greatly praised and told that my fortune was made. Maybe thought I, but what use if I'm killed. However, there's nothing wrong, my snake may be good, and I may escape. Laying down my shield, and taking off my dress, I crept in on my belly, having asked those outside to make a great noise, so that my movements should not be heard. I went along very quietly, with my spear in my hand till I felt the feet of the dead man who had gone before me. I lifted him up very gently, and 'swarmed' along until I had got him fairly on my back; then with him in that position, I went on for about my own length, and felt stab, stab, thud, thud, as they ran assegais into his body and struck him with sticks. I shouted 'Maie' (oh, dear), groaned and gave a wriggle or two, then lay still. It was quite dark, and all was quiet outside. Immediately someone said, 'That is the third; move the stone and let us see him,' and one stepped over me in obedience to the command. I grasped my assegai, and, just as the first light came in by the opening he was making, I sprang up and stabbed him, shouting at the same time to our people, 'In with you, in with you,' and, turning, defended myself from those who were in the entrance. I had only to do so for a few moments. Our people came rushing in, and I escaped with a few cuts. By this time we could hear the hum of the alarmed Amaswazi, like bees in a hole; so like was it, that the instantaneous cry was, 'Let us dig out this honey-nest, it is fat,' but our officers made us wait for more force; it came, and we went forward. We walked along a good way on a fine grassy glade, a stream of water running through the centre, and the rocks nearly meeting overhead, until at last we came to a large circular piece of ground – as large as the flat outside there (say a mile in diameter), a waterfall at one end, precipices all around, and wood here and there about the foot of them, but not a soul was to be seen. We hunted until at last we found many openings into caves at the sides, and these we at once stormed, our whole force having by this time come up. The people within fought well, and we were hunting one another but we got lights, and then we finished them off.

Did we kill the women and children, say you? Ay, that we did. Why not? The children would grow up into soldiers to fight us, and the women would bear more.

I came to one girl. As I raised my assegai she looked at me, clasped her hands over her eyes, and said 'Ow um-ta-ka-baba' (oh child of my father, my brother); that was all, and, do you know, I could not kill her. Chaka! I couldn't (swears by his King). She had 'medicine' that girl. I had killed that day till my assegai was blunt and my arm was weary, but all anger seemed to go out at my fingers and toes. So I said, 'Rise, Tdadte (sister), no one will hurt you.' I defended her from others. Many would have attacked me, but I was always recognized in time as the brave who had gained the entrance, and the cry was, 'Let him alone; let him keep the girl.' 'Ah, but,' cried others, 'he'll have to give her up to the King.' Then for the first time, I remembered the orders, and I looked up to see if I had not come suddenly under a waterfall. I turned towards the girl; she was gazing on the ground. 'Lulama' (straighten yourself) I cried. Our eyes met. Something seemed to soften and melt, warmly and gradually, within me. I began to be disgusted with the blood which covered me. I thought of my sisters and my mother at home, and I thought of her father and mother, most likely killed that day. Somehow or other it came into my mind that she was alone and in sorrow, and would be torn from her country and her people, and given to be a slave to the King, for no fault of her own; and still I warmed and melted, until at last I became a child, and determined to save her from our army, and send her back to her folk, if, haply, any were alive. I tell you, she had medicine, that girl. I took her quietly to one side, and said, 'Look here! I must give you up to the officers for the King; but watch; be quick to understand what I say or do, and I'll find an opportunity of letting you go safely.' She did not answer – she only looked at me; but something in the look was better than spoken words. Well, when all was over, we gathered together our cattle and our captives, ready for our homeward march; and by way of reward I was appointed an officer of the guard of the latter, just what I would have wished for. We travelled for a day without being able to exchange a word with the 'Swazi girl, though I wanted to, very much; I felt just as if I was hungry. She was somewhere in the centre of the throng, and has told me since that she kept edging outwards, until she got close to where I was, hoping that I would, yet fearing that I would not, address her. When I saw her near I began to look about for an opening to let her go. I made a sign to keep close by me. She did so; and towards dusk, as we were marching by a wooded ravine, I managed to give her a push. She sprang clear in, and I purposely fell in the way of the man behind who was jumping in after her. She got away, the more easily, as I shouted to my men to stand firm and guard those who were left, in case they should go too. I thought I had managed so cleverly; but I was to hear more of it, as you shall see. I would have been killed, only my snake stood straight up.

We reported to the generals the loss of the captive; they said it could not be helped, and spoke of something else. We travelled on without further adventure until we got near the King's again; when we halted, and messengers were sent forward to announce our return. A day was appointed for a review at Nodwengo, and we all brushed ourselves up to look our best. The day came. We defiled before the great one, and each had our little praise; then came the giving out of the cattle. A great many had received their rewards, when the cry was raised for the brave who had gained the entrance to show himself, and I had to step forward. 'To me,' said the King, 'you have shown yourself a soldier indeed, and deserving of a King's notice; there is a troop of cattle for you. But –, now I shall kill you for helping one of the captive girls escape. What say you?' I saw it was no use attempting to get out of the hobble, so I spoke boldly. I knew that kings like those who speak out, but I trembled all the while.

'Yes, father; yes, wild beast; yes, you that are black,' I replied. 'The King is, of course, right. I ought to be killed; but I could not help it. She bewitched me.' 'How so?' asked he; and I told him the whole affair, with all the symptoms. When I had done, he burst out laughing, and said, 'Hau! the idiot fell in love with her. Go, go; you are a brave soldier, but a fool in these matters. I should have

thought a young man of your age and appearance would have known more. Hau! the fool! What was it like? Tell me of it. Was it painful?'

'No, father, I can't say it was painful. It was like a sickness though. It was just 'Umhlolo' (unnatural and inexplicable). 'Go, go,' he said. 'You have escaped.' I went quickly, took my cattle, and thanked my snake all the way home. That was the beginning of my rise; till now, as you see me, I have many kraals, much people, and plenty cattle.

Well, when I had been at home for about ten days, I went paying visits all round, was everywhere praised and fed; but still something was wanting. My heart continually ached with a dull pain. I felt a want. At night I dreamt about the 'Swazi girl. By day I thought of her. I saw her face in the burning coals of fire. I halted while eating my food to think of her, until my people said 'How much that young man speaks to his heart' (thinks). I went hunting but I used to forget what I was about. In the dance I would stop and not know it. Hau! that love is an Umhlolo indeed.

At last, one morning while lying lost in my hut, my sisters came rushing in, saying that they had found a girl half-dead with cold in the garden, and that she was Swazi by her tongue. My heart leapt up at once and with it my body. I knew it was she. It was as if something was drawing me with a rope. The girls laughed; they had a shrewd idea as to what was the matter. I ran out and there I found her: pinched with hunger, shrivelled with cold, done with weariness; but yet with the same glancing look I remembered in the cave. I spoke to her; asked her where she came from, and why she had left her own people. She crossed her arms upon her breasts, burst into tears, and, as she was falling to the ground, I caught her up and carried her to my kraal. On the way she told me, 'My people were all killed; who was I to go to? Our kraals were burnt; where was I to live? I thought of you, and said, I will go to him who spared me in the great slaughter; I will hoe his corn, and cook his food, and –' what more she said does not matter now; but there is the old woman beside you, and sometimes I think she has medicine still.

'At first when I heard the old song
I listened bitter, ignorant,
But now in a new light I make amends.
When your voices murmur in your breasts
Echoing from the depths of old passions,
Carried from the Zulu hills out across
    the earth,
They call back to me things that are
    no more,
Faint almost beyond grope of memory
And the long river of my tears.'

I Heard the Old Song
B.W. Vilakazi
The Penguin Book of South African Verse.
Edited by Jack Cope and Uys Krige.

GREAT RHINOCEROS

'The two white rhinoceros which I shot in 1882 are the last of their species that I have ever seen alive, or am ever likely to see and when I left Africa towards the end of 1892 I fully expected that these animals would become extinct within a short time.'

Frederick Courteny Selous –
African Nature Notes and Reminiscences

There he was – antediluvian, massive and dangerous looking, rising suspiciously to his feet in a cloud of disturbed flies – a solitary mud-plastered black rhino bull, as compact and uncompromising as a battering ram. Long-hulked, his grey hide, like saggy vulcanized rubber, haemorrhaged from raw pink lesions on his chest and flanks. Heavily wrinkled snout, flared nostrils and a pointed prehensile top lip that looked like a finger beneath an anterior horn that canted forward a little then curved gently upwards to a wicked point, he batted a shredded left ear, setting the flies off again, then swivelled his armoured uncomprehending head – the movement bringing broadside a murky eye that reflected light beyond the range of his vision. A redbilled oxpecker probed one of his nostrils in search of ticks but the rhino ignored the intrusion. He stood in the filtered shade of a buffalo thorn on bare brown earth that proclaimed it a favourite rest site – silent and unmoving, like a great rough-hewn granite boulder, pored over by chirring brown birds. Solid, indestructible, eternal; he looked in the clean soft light the ugliest, most magnificent sight imaginable.

It was my first meeting with one of Umfolozi's black rhinos, two days after I had arrived. I was alone and on foot as were nearly all my subsequent encounters, as the rhinos are far too shy to permit an approach by motor vehicle.

I welcomed the opportunity of doing without a car – the only way to know wild country is to walk it and although there is a risk in going unarmed and on foot among big game, a knowledge of their habits and temperament makes it not an unduly hazardous proposition. Anyway I have, for several years now, rejected the notion of living cautiously. The stimulation of being at risk makes worthwhile the potential penalties and a charging black rhino is one of the best remedies against boredom I know.

Umfolozi-Hluhluwe is in many people's minds synonymous with rhinos. Both the smaller, browsing hook-lipped or black rhinoceros and the huge grazing square-lipped or white rhinoceros reside here in abundance. Hluhluwe has the highest density of black rhinos in Africa while adjoining Umfolozi has the highest density of white, although the two occur throughout the complex. I went with the intention of taking a close look at both species – as close, that is, as their uncertain tempers permitted.

There is something strangely compelling about this fractious protean pachyderm as he arranges his shambling dignity around him and proceeds on his affairs much as his ancestors did seven hundred thousand centuries ago. At one time or another there were as many as 170 species and millions of years ago rhinos even roamed the forests of southern England. Now there are only five species left – the great Indian one-horned, Javan and Sumatran rhinos of Asia and the black and white rhinos of Africa.

The black rhino is the most numerous of the five, but in the last few years it has been the one most heavily poached and most East African populations have been drastically reduced. Kenya, in the last ten years, has lost over 90 per cent of its rhinos. Towards the middle of 1982 Tanzania raised a corps of 1 000 militiamen in a belated attempt to save what remained of a rapidly dwindling national herd. Poachers, many of them arriving from Somalia with Russian arms accumulated from the war in the Ogaden, have spread across and into the depths of East Africa.

The conservation of the black rhino by the Natal Parks Board has not attracted the sort of attention given to its more acclaimed work in saving the white, but it is equally important. Indeed it is thanks to the Natal Parks' efforts that the black rhino survived at all in South Africa. By 1945 it had become extinct throughout the country except for an estimated 100 in Hluhluwe, Umfolozi and Mkuzi game reserves. Once their strict protection had been ensured they responded with a gradual but steady increase.

Conservationists expressed jubilation after a census in Hluhluwe in February 1961 revealed 300 black rhino where previously they had been estimated at just over 200. However the unusually high densities in a species that is asocial due to the relative scarcity of its food, precipitated a 15 per cent die-off the same year. Thirty-five animals were captured and removed to relieve the pressure but the population continued to decline in a density-dependent way.

Fights between male and female black rhinos during courtship vary in seriousness according to the individuals involved. Here, a black rhino bull pursues a cow that he had been mating with moments before. In this instance the bull's attack was sufficiently vicious to lacerate the cow's foreleg and reduce her to pitiful squeals. However, no sooner was his vindictiveness dissipated than he returned to his courtship with the cow's not too grudging co-operation.

The shortage of suitable browse was due to management-induced habitat changes introduced to combat bush encroachment. With the removal of large numbers of predominantly grazing animals, improved grassland conditions supported fierce bushfires that invaded and reduced acacia thickets on which the black rhino relied. At present Hluhluwe's population is kept static by translocating excess animals to other parks where they once roamed.

My first encounter with a black rhino contained all the elements with which I was to become familiar without ever taking them for granted. There is always, on first sighting, a decided quickening of the pulse, an intense prickle of expectation and heightened awareness, the knowledge that the situation has gone beyond one's control – what happens next depends on the rhino.

I had seen him from the crest of Mbulunga Ridge in Umfolozi as he went about his disultory browsing in the Gqoyini catchment below. I dribbled a handful of dust through my fingers to divine the wind direction. A rhino's vision and hearing is poor but it has an acute sense of smell and it is olfactory stimuli which make up the greatest part of its external world. Therefore, I had to stalk him downwind and rely on his myopia to go undetected.

The excitable, unpredictable temperament of the black rhino contrasts strongly with the inoffensive nature of the white. This is highlighted by the black's tendency to rush suddenly towards an intruder uttering three steam engine-like chuffs as it does so – all of which helps to create a frightening impression. Its belligerence is one of the reasons the black rhino does not have many friends in the world.

It is considered a stupid ill-tempered brute that attacks at the slightest provocation; nor is it furry, cuddly or charis-

matic. People have trouble relating to it and a recent appeal by the World Wildlife Fund for contributions to a 'Save the Rhino' campaign fared badly. The rhino's poor public image dates back to its first contacts with early explorers and hunters. 'A meddling officious marplot', complained gentleman-hunter Cornwallis Harris, 'perpetually in the way, and always prepared for mischief, wheresoever the rhinoceros was not required, there he was sure to be.'

W H Drummond incorrectly believed, in common with many other hunters of the time, that there were four species of rhino, two white and two black, which were distinguished by different horn sizes. He described the one black rhino as being 'the smallest, most savage, and most to be dreaded. . . Sufficient anecdotes of its ferocity, chronic bad temper and cunning might be related of themselves to fill a volume. Their cunning is only equalled by their viciousness. . .

When wounded, and occasionally when much disturbed, their spoor consists of parallel straight lines, so that it is next to impossible to overtake them without being discovered, and giving them an opportunity of charging you from one side. They will wait with the utmost patience, concealed in thick jungle, and then rush out at you. When they do catch an unfortunate being, they knock him down, and knead him with their feet, returning again and again until nothing but a shapeless mass remains, uttering all the day their shrill squeal of rage. This I once saw myself.'

Old hunters' tales such as this are a blend of fact, fancy and misunderstanding or incorrect interpretation of what has taken place. Being near-sighted almost to the point of blindness, black rhinos spend much of their lives in a state of myopic confusion — reacting with false alarms to imagined dangers and often in benign ignorance of real ones. If they be-

come aware of a vague presence they are liable to rush forward to investigate and on discovering a potential enemy they may either charge or run for their lives which, at close quarters, may be mistaken for a charge. Where rhinos have been thought to be waiting in ambush is almost certainly an unexpected encounter in thick bush where they spend much of their time feeding and into which they retreat when alarmed. The surprise is mutual and the rhino responds in the only way it knows how – by attacking.

My pleasure at this intimate sharing of the rhino's space was dispelled by a sudden shift of wind. He reacted immediately – lofting his head – hesitated a moment, then broke into terror-stricken flight away from me. So panicked was he that he didn't stop running until well out of sight in some thick bush. It is generally held to be true that a black rhino will, on scenting man, charge upwind in an effort to locate him, yet, on subse-

quent encounters, I never found this to be the case. White rhinos on the other hand often pull up after a short retreat and turn about to face in the direction they have come. Groups will sometimes form a defensive circle, standing rump to rump, each facing in a different direction.

Before leaving for Zululand, a good friend of mine from our days together in Etosha, Garth Owen-Smith, recommended I contact his brother Norman, who had spent nearly six years in Umfolozi studying the white rhino's social system for his doctoral thesis.

We met on the campus of Witwatersrand University in the neatly ordered cubicle he occupied in one of the new functional wings. Motioning me to a seat, he gestured about him with a melancholy acceptance: 'I get out into the bush as often as I can – at least once or twice a month.' Traffic noises poured in through an open window. A black-and-white photograph of two white rhino bulls in a horn against horn territorial dispute, backlit by disturbed dust, caught my attention. Where it had been taken seemed very far away indeed.

I had told him earlier that I wanted to photograph aspects of rhino social behaviour and hoped he could give me some advice. He leant back reflectively, his words receding into the background of urban babble, then spoke in a soft voice that belied the intensity with which he approached his favourite subject. I hitched forward and indicated the black-and-white photograph on his desk.

'That sort of shot.'

Norman tipped back his head and laughed. 'Well then,' he said, composing himself, 'I'd better warn you, patience is a prerequisite.'

Rhinos, as I had suspected and Norman was quick to confirm, are notoriously non-demonstrative. They eat, they sleep. Their social system is organized to minimize interspecific confrontations between potentially lethal protagonists. Their size and willingness to put their horns to effective use means that adult rhinos are all but invulnerable to predation except from man. They do not miss the safety in numbers advantage which social groups enjoy. In fact rhinos stand at the least social end of the large herbivore spectrum. With so little

interaction taking place I would need to spend long hours waiting for something to happen, which, as Norman pointed out with a small smile, would usually result in their rushing off once they had detected me.

There was probably no better person in the world to talk to about white rhinos than Norman Owen-Smith. His unsentimental forthright approach to their future welfare is as refreshing as it is practical. He was able to answer all my questions, even those I had not thought to pose. He supplied me with copies of his research papers, walked me to the elevator and wished me luck.

A month had passed before I actually arrived in the Gqoyini catchment where I had decided to concentrate my activities. Its open parkland savanna of red oat grass *(Themeda triandra)* interspersed with that typically African tree, the umbrella thorn *(Acacia tortilis)* attracted large numbers of rhinos and other species.

In the months that followed, I came to know by sight all the rhinos that lived there and spent many relaxed hours in their company. In a landscape free of useless motion they personified that economy of movement. A rhino under a tree at mid-day is the epitome of repose with only its fringed funnel-shaped ears twitching and an occasional deep exhalation, like a heartfelt sigh, that raises a sudden puff of fine dust.

I once watched a territorial white rhino bull through my binoculars as he methodically plucked with broad lips the short-cropped grass close to ground-level. He grazed with imperturbable self-confidence, forging slowly ahead, never stopping to check for danger. He was inviolate, the largest land mammal in the world after the elephant and perhaps the largest entirely grass-feeding herbivore ever to have evolved.

At one point he wiped his anterior horn sideways over a low bush, then dragged his hindlegs stiffly over the site before curling his tail out of the way and directing a fine shower of urine in four powerful spasmodic bursts over the scrapes. Only territorial bulls scent-mark by ritualized spray-urinating in this way. Rhino urine has an acrid lingering smell.

Rhinos tend to defecate where other rhino dung is already present, so that large dung heaps – called middens – are

A black rhino scent-marks by directing a fine shower of urine in spasmodic bursts onto a shrub. Only dominant bulls practise ritualized spray-urinating in this way to announce their presence to other rhinos. Above right, a bull raises his head and pulls back his top lip in a 'flehmen' grimace on sniffing the urine of an oestrous cow. This action facilitates the analysis (by smell and taste) of the urine's hormone content, signalling to the bull a female's readiness to breed. Rhinos are remarkable in that copulation lasts 30 minutes or even longer compared to the few seconds most animals take. The calf watching the proceedings will remain with the cow until another calf is born. Immediately on dismounting the bull attacked the cow and a brief, fierce scuffle ensued. However, field biologists report that, where post-copulatory attacks occur, it is usually the cow that is the aggressor.

A territorial white rhino bull squares off against subordinate bulls who respond with defensive 'snarl-threats' and loud, rasping roars. Encounters between territorial bulls and subordinates are non-violent and brief; once the dominant male has reinforced his status he moves on.

a feature of their habitat. Dominant bulls also use these middens as signposts to demarcate their territories by kicking backwards to break up and scatter their dung over the heap so that their smell is dominant. Middens with centres hollowed out by this kicking action are a sign of a territorial bull's presence and are concentrated along borders.

Until Dr Norman Owen-Smith's study rhinos were thought by some biologists to be non-territorial as the home ranges of adult bulls can overlap considerably. Whereas this overlap certainly occurs, Owen-Smith was able to show that while dominant bulls occupy mutually exclusive territories averaging two square kilometres year-round, about one-third of the adult males are merely subordinates and therefore not territory owners. Each of these subordinate bulls co-inhabits the territory of one of the territorial bulls but unlike him, they may wander outside their home range. They use the same middens as the dominant bull, but neither scatter their dung nor spray their urine.

One morning I watched as a territorial white rhino bull approached three subordinates. They stood their ground, uttering loud roars and snarls, heads thrust

forward, ears back and tails tightly curled. Their intimidatory gestures were defensive threats, the same as those employed by cows and adolescents towards a territorial bull. The bull walked forward and briefly fenced with one of the subordinates who gave a trumpeting shriek. The bull then nonchalantly disengaged and wondered off, leaving the three subordinates standing.

Should a territorial bull be deposed, he is not driven off his territory but is allowed to remain with the down-graded status of a subordinate. Later he may try to gain possession of a neighbouring one. A defeated territorial bull immediately ceases spray urination and more gradually dung scattering.

Adult cows restrict their movements, if conditions are good, to a home range encompassing six to seven male territories although a territorial bull will confine an oestrous cow on his territory for up to two weeks. Subordinate bulls do not form such consort relationships and play no part in reproduction.

An interesting experience I had with a white rhino tended to bear out one of the more unlikely behavioural traits attributed by Baldwin to the black rhino when he claimed that 'they will at once

For all their easy-going ways, white rhinos brook no nonsense from lesser species, even one so potentially lethal as this outcast buffalo bull – it was the buffalo that eventually retreated.

charge on getting the wind of a human being and if they cross his track, they will often follow it up like a dog, making none of the puffing sounds natural to them when angry, till they absolutely sight him.'

I had been following undetected a white rhino cow and her sub-adult calf as they slowly grazed their way along a well-worn game trail when they met up with another cow and calf in the company of a mature bull. After a brief horn to horn greeting ceremony, the five moved off together down the trail that I was coming up. I backed off, keeping a distance of about 50 metres between us. Before long they reached where I had last been standing and responded instantly. Flared nostrils filled with human smell, they wheeled to left and right in a frantic attempt to locate their only natural enemy. The cows and calves broke off at a right angle to me but the bull, to my astonishment, came shuffling on down the trail, nose close to the ground, ears pricked forward, like a preposterous bloodhound.

Wondering how long he would keep this up I retreated before him as quietly as possible, dodging from one climbable tree to the next. Incredibly he stayed on

my spoor for 120 metres, as I later paced out, and would have done so for longer if the gap between us had not been narrowing, prompting me to scramble up a marula tree. My pursuer pulled up beneath me – I could have stepped on his back – and gazed around, looking, I thought, a little baffled. Then his nerve broke and tail curled tightly over his back he barrelled off with that characteristic stiff-legged rhino jog. After such a virtuoso performance I almost felt like applauding though probably I would have reacted quite differently if he had tracked me without my knowledge.

Which is one of the problems rhino admirers have – their fond approbation is never reciprocated. The late John Goddard, who studied rhinos in Kenya and Zambia spoke up in their defense, saying it is 'a shortsighted, harmless old beast that deserves. . . the greatest degree of sympathy you can give it.' It certainly does deserve sympathy, but equally certain it is not harmless.

In 1871 a son of the Zulu king Mpande died and as was the custom a great iHlambo hunt was organized, accompanied by the ceremonial washing of the spears, so that by the act of shedding blood the warriors could purify them-

selves and the nation from the defilement of his death. One of the largest regiments, the Tulwane, numbering about 2 000 men, came upon a notorious black rhino known to have caused the deaths of seven people. The pugnacious beast, undaunted by the mob, immediately charged, causing a general flight. This was only momentary however; the impi rallied and battle was joined. After killing four of the braves and seriously wounding several others the rhino finally succumbed, its body bristling with imbedded assegais. That classic confrontation between man and rhino defines in its essence the relationship between the two. Small wonder rhinos are irascible.

Rhinos are not hostile to all creatures – they have a symbiotic fellowship with several, based on their heavy tick load. The most important of these are the red-billed oxpeckers that daily gobble up a prodigious number of ticks and blood-sucking flies. I have also seen them eat the crusted blood from the open lesions that all adult black rhinos have, caused by infestations of tiny, whitish, thread-like microfilarial parasites.

Oxpeckers prefer the two species of rhino more than any other host, followed by buffalo and giraffe. The gregarious

Opposite. On getting our scent white rhinos would often pull up after a short retreat and turn about to face in the direction whence they had come. Groups sometimes form a defensive circle, standing rump to rump, each facing in a different direction. Black rhinos, however, stampeded away in terror-stricken flight, not stopping till they disappeared from sight into heavy bush. Although it is generally held to be true that a black rhino will, on scenting man, charge upwind in an effort to locate him, we never found this to be the case.

A browsing black rhino, above, uses her prehensile upper lip to grasp vegetation and then manoeuvre it into her mouth. Black rhinos are highly selective and very partial to small ground plants that erupt in the wake of late summer rains. A white rhino's broad square mouth and straight upper lip is designed for cropping. Here, above right, it is put to equally good use chewing the mineral-enriched soil that excavating termites have brought to the surface.

noisy birds also act as efficient early-warning systems, alerting rhinos to danger with a harsh, chirring alarm call – a sinister sound, reminiscent of the ominous rattle used in action movies to heighten tension as the hero moves into the danger zone. Initially I was puzzled when, in spite of a favourable prevailing wind and in the absence of oxpeckers, a rhino would nevertheless sometimes become apprehensive as I crept up. Only later did I realize that they also react to the alarm calls of birds not associating directly with them, in particular the strident little cisticolas.

Glossy starlings and forktailed drongos often follow rhinos, sometimes riding on their backs then swooping down to snatch up insects disturbed by their monumental feet. I have seen a drongo flying beating sorties along the flanks of a sleeping white rhino, starting up the swarms of bloodsucking flies that cluster there, then hawking them on the wing.

The ubiquitous pied crow, that raffish lovable character, its eye ever cocked to the main chance, has extended its already impressive feeding niche to include ectoparasites plucked off tolerant large mammals. I thought it little short of ludicrous to see it telling off the cock-

eyed world atop a rhino's head, its harsh unrefined voice the perfect medium with which to deliver the message. It then marched self-importantly down the rhino's spine to probe for ticks under its tail. When the rhino was moving, it had trouble maintaining its balance, not having the curved claws of the more highly specialized oxpeckers. Ectoparasites are not an important food source to crows so it did not spend much of each day in rhino company.

During the hot summer months rhinos spend long hours wallowing in rainwater pans. I had made a hide in the shade of a Transvaal gardenia (*Gardenia spatulifolia*) adjacent to one of these pans and watched as, late one afternoon the local territorial black rhino bull approached. He came down as brusque as ever until he reached the water's edge, then a transformation took place – he dropped his snout into the ooze, pushed it along, then raised it up, savouring the pleasure to come before giving himself over to the hedonism of the bath.

The freshwater turtles – terrapins – crowded round, snapping up ticks with great gusto. The rhino flinched when they took occasional nibbles at the bloody lesions on his body, then settled

A rhino's hide provides a pasture of parasites for a surprising variety of symbionts. Redbilled oxpeckers swarm over this white rhino cow and calf while a pied crow, overleaf, top left, stretches to peck crusted blood from the open lesions caused by microfalarial parasites found on all adult Zululand black rhinos.

again immediately, to allow the grooming to continue.

With so many symbionts benefiting from their association with a rhino, the huge animal becomes virtually a mobile ecosystem unto itself. Nor does a rhino's importance to the lives and wellbeing of lesser creatures end there.

Rhino middens figure in the environment of many species which either visit or live in them. Of the invertebrate community living in the heap, the most obvious are the dungbeetles; in the humid summer months when they are most active the heap appears to be a heaving mass as hundreds collect and roll away balls of dung. Eggs are deposited in the ball, which is then buried a metre underground and when the eggs hatch the developing larvae feed on the dung.

Flies, butterflies and other insects are also attracted by the fresh dung; some to feed, others to lay eggs in it. Insectivorous birds and mammals take advantage of the concentrated food supply offered by so many invertebrate residents. Banded mongoose, shrews, moles and aardwolfs forage for beetle larvae while crowned guinea fowl, crested and Natal francolin, hadedahs and redwinged glossy starlings scratch after morsels. Harvester termites cart away undigested grass stems to their nests. So quite unwittingly a rhino leaves a rather comprehensive natural cycle in its wake.

On one of my early walks I came across the collapsed shell of a white rhino carcass in the Gqoyini Valley, the rigid punctured hide draped over the

A forktailed drongo, above, flies beating sorties along the flank of a sleeping white rhino, starting up the swarms of bloodsucking flies that gather there, then hawks them on the wing.

Opposite. A terrapin or freshwater turtle snaps a tick off the snout of a wallowing rhino. No sooner had the rhino settled in this pan than the resident terrapins crowded around, making him flinch whenever they nibbled at the lesions on his flank but he quickly relaxed again, allowing the grooming to continue. Rhino dung middens feature in the environment of many decomposers which either visit or live in them. Mushrooms are the fruit bodies of large fungi which depend on complex substances in order to complete their life-cycles. Dungbeetles collect and roll away balls of dung for future food supplies and nests, then bury them a metre underground, thus manure is injected directly into the earth.

Rhinos are easy animals to stalk and kill. The 2 000 years since rhino horn came into fashion has not provided them enough time to evolve a defence against the one predator that hunts them more widely, efficiently and wastefully than any other. Rhinos have been hunted in Africa since the early hominids first applied their expanded intelligence and manipulative hands to fashion sharp bones into spears.

When Cornwallis Harris penetrated the southern African interior 150 years ago, the Stone Age Khoisan bushmen had already been largely supplanted by Iron Age Bantu pastoralists able to organize large-scale collective hunts. Rhinos were nonetheless still 'extremely abundant' in spite of the fact that 'the savage natives of Africa who regard neither species with much dread, wage a successful war against them with the assegai; and pitfalls containing pointed stakes, constructed purposely for the accommodation of the unwieldly beasts were of very frequent occurrence. Strewed with huge skulls and bones they differed from those excavated for the smaller quadrupeds in being dug singly, instead of in groups – of increased dimensions – at the extremity of a narrow path cleared through the bushes and stoutly fenced on either side with thorns; a sharp turn leading so directly upon the hidden sepulchre, that the clumsy monster, if driven furiously down the avenue, can have little chance of evading it.'

At the same time as Harris was in the field, Nathaniel Isaacs was visiting Zululand and carefully recording all he saw there. 'Hunting is a favourite amusement with the Zoolas,' he wrote, 'and it is a profitable one. They are expert and dauntless in their pursuit of the elephant, which they attack with great intrepidity. The rhinoceros approaches the elephant in point of strength, but being a remarkably heavy, stupid, inert animal,

splayed skeleton, a dislocated jawbone with great corrugated molars still in place. It served as a useful if obvious symbol of the alternatives. In the poacher's savage war of attrition against Africa's embattled wildlife, nothing is sacred and the rhino is bearing the brunt of it. For all their dim-witted obtuseness, rhinos remain immensely fragile and mysterious. The prehistoric ponderous placid 'white' and its combustible cousin live by no one else's rules – they are unique and a world without them would have lost one of its subtleties.

The present poaching onslaught is due to an increased demand for rhino horn on the world market, not only for the traditional medicinal trade in the Far East, but also for the North Yemen market where the horns are carved into dagger handles. The world market has consumed nearly eight tonnes of rhino horn annually in recent years, for which about 2 660 rhinos were killed every year. Because of the growing demand, the price has increased some 2 000 per cent reaching a minimum wholesale price of US $750 per kilo in South-East Asia. Such prices are naturally a great incentive to poaching.

the hunters have no risk or difficulty in killing him.'

In the millennia since the emergence of *Australopithecus* man-apes to thriving Bantu settlements and despite increasingly sophisticated hunting methods, the African rhinos had never been in danger of extermination. That threat began only with the advent of firearms, long-range instruments of death to which the rhino in particular was vulnerable.

The placid southern white rhinoceros originally ranged throughout the bushveld regions of the Transvaal, Moçambique, Botswana, Namibia, Angola, Zimbabwe, Swaziland and Zululand. It stepped into the scientific limelight one crisp Kalahari spring day in October 1812 near Kuruman when William John Burchell, by far the greatest of the early African naturalists, recognized it as a new species of rhino. He promptly shot 10 specimens from which to obtain his data. Others were soon to follow his example so that almost from the time of the white rhino's description by Burchell the elimination from its extensive range began.

By 1880 it had disappeared from the northern Cape, Namibia and Botswana; in 1896 from Zimbabwe, and in the Transvaal that same year the last one was shot in an area that would later become the Kruger National Park, making the white rhino, according to James Steven-

son-Hamilton, the first and only species completely lost to the Transvaal lowveld, although by no later than 1945 it had been joined by the black rhino. At the turn of the century all that remained of the white rhinoceros in Moçambique were bleached knuckles, heaps of vertebrae and cracked, hollow-eyed skulls. In 80 years it had been reduced to no more than 30 animals – about as close to extinction as anything can get – closeted on a 250 square-kilometre V-shaped wedge of land between the two branches of the Umfolozi River in Zululand.

The happy conclusion to the white rhino saga is intimately tied up with the history of Umfolozi Game Reserve. Without the one the other would no longer exist. With its creation in 1897 Umfolozi became a sanctuary for the last survivors and its status as such enabled conservationists to head off repeated calls for its deproclamation.

In the decade immediately following Umfolozi's creation the protection of wildlife was scanty. Then in 1911 Frederick Vaughn-Kirby was appointed as the first Game Conservator for Zululand. Vaughn-Kirby was a stern preservationist; lean, with a ramrod carriage, thinning silver hair, bristling eyebrows, crows feet at the corners of eyes, long slitted against the African sun, and a clipped military moustache. He had a fiery

temper and a supreme distrust of man's motives where wildlife was concerned.

He was imbued with a missionary zeal to be the personal and single-handed saviour of Umfolozi's slowly recovering herds. He had seen too much abuse and neglect of wildlife resources to trust anyone else. His closest white neighbours were farmers, one of whom said of him; 'We have suffered from a game conservator who thought of nothing but preservation and whose sole idea was to prevent the slaughter of a single animal.' Feeling pressed on all sides the crusty conservator responded with a lonely crusade of well-intentioned deception.

In 1922 he gave the white rhino population to be only 25 or 26; a deliberate under-estimate to emphasize their precarious situation. Then in 1929 his subterfuge was penetrated. In response to farmers' complaints that Umfolozi's game herds acted as hosts to the tsetse fly which spread a fatal trypanosomiasis amongst their cattle, the provincial council sent a team under a man called Harris to conduct an intensive campaign of driving game from the boundaries of the settlements into the sanctuary. Soon after his arrival Harris discovered that Vaughn-Kirby's white rhino figures were grossly inaccurate. He was told by the game guards that there were in reality between 150 and 180 animals and that Vaughn-

Poaching of rhinos for their horns has reached epidemic proportions throughout much of Africa. This calf has lost its hindfoot in a cable snare and, though maimed, it managed to escape – many do not. Snares are devices of grotesque cleverness and cruelty and laying them is a particularly indiscriminate way of poaching. While some do their best to push rhinos into extinction, others,

bottom, are doing all they can to rescue them. When, in the early 1960s, overgrazing in the Zululand parks threatened rhino habitat the Natal Parks Board responded by immobilizing and translocating surplus animals. In the 20 years since, 3 200 white and 100 black rhinos out of a grand total of 54 000 animals have been captured live and moved to depleted areas.

Kirby had in fact organized a ground count shortly before Harris arrived.

'This information,' said Harris in astonishment, 'in the light of what the world has been led to believe appeared so staggering that I instructed Ranger Werner at once to make a very careful check of the number of white rhinoceros in each section of the sanctuary. He was instructed to take the greatest care not to count any of the animals over and particularly to note the sex, length and shape of horns and the colour of the mud in which the animals had wallowed.'

The recount revealed that there were probably no less than 200 white rhino in the park. When Vaughn-Kirby's duplicity was brought to the attention of a Mr C Clarkson, the provincial councillor responsible for wildlife affairs, the honourable member exploded.

'The disparity between the present estimate and that previously published can only be explained by the grossly inadequate way in which the Administration has been served by certain of its employees in the past. There has never before been any reason to doubt the estimates of game furnished by the officials on the spot and steps have been taken to see that it cannot occur again.'

Vaughn-Kirby was finished. He re-

Rhinos stand at the least social end of the large herbivore spectrum, all but invulnerable to predation except from man.

fused to back down though, preferring to go out defiantly. In an open letter to Clarkson published in the Natal Witness (Est 27 Feb 1846 to 'stand as a witness in matters of public interest!') the editor 'found it necessary to remove from the letter, as originally received, certain passages the publication of which, it was considered, would have been an infringement of the law.'

'You have the impertinence,' Vaughn-Kirby thundered, 'to say that the Administration was 'badly served' because forsooth I did not as you allege, count the white rhinoceros correctly! It yet remains to be seen how near to correctly Harris and his gang (carefully wrapped up in cottonwool to protect them from climatic vagaries) have made the count.'

Werner had made no mistake. The white rhino population had increased dramatically and from this nucleus all existing representatives of the southern race have been derived. As they multiplied there arose a danger that they would outstrip their food supply by overgrazing the grasslands. However a plan to transfer the excess animals to former ranges in southern Africa became feasible in the early 1960s with the development of safe and potent immobilizing drugs. Once the drugs and capture techniques had been proved successfully, the Natal Parks Board began exporting white rhinos to zoos in many parts of the world and recolonizing game parks where they had once occurred.

Today more than 3 000 white rhino have been translocated – a spectacular retreat from the abyss of extinction. In 1965 the International Union for the Conservation of Nature was able to declare the animal had been saved, and it was removed from the Class A Protection List – the only creature ever to have achieved that distinction. Threatened habitats probably pose the greatest danger to animal extinction the world over.

UMFOLOZI

*'The buffalo is enquired about
from those who go ahead.'*
Zulu Proverb

Viewed from the heights of Msaseneni the open woodlands and riverine forests of this north-western corner of Umfolozi spread away, shrouded by rising dust particles that reduced all colours to a wash of greys, browns and pastel greens, as though seen through a dirty gauze curtain. The land looked dry and sun-bleached; the white heat awesome. It ricocheted off the rocks and stubbled earth to collect in deep incandescent pools. There was no movement in the valley below – as if all life had withdrawn to the shadows. A lone eagle floated slowly across the empty sky, its cry, filled with falsetto intensity, served only to add to an aroused sense of foreboding.

The scene was all wrong for this time of the year. It was early March and the wet season should have been drawing to a close but after a promising start the rains had tapered off, then ceased altogether. All through January and February not a drop had fallen; the grass that had shot up so confidently stood stunted and tawny, rattling in the wind.

The summer drought was disastrous and everyone I had spoken to was deeply worried. Umfolozi had experienced enough desiccation for people to have an acute awareness of how bad the consequences could be. The drought of the early 1980s had precipitated a major overgrazing problem resulting in bare, capped earth and an increased rate of soil erosion, to say nothing of the wildlife that died of starvation once the grass had disappeared.

The game park was in a 'rain shadow' surrounded on all sides by higher rainfall areas. Although average annual precipitation is 700 millimetres, it can vary considerably from year to year. When I went there, in late summer, heavy afternoon thunderstorms were usual and their failure was sorely missed.

Running the length of Msaseneni ridge is a well-established rhino trail that sensibly follows the easiest gradients in that hilly, broken country. It is well defined with an even, smooth surface, obviously used by every kind of animal and I was no exception. All such paths gradually converge on water and this one, holding to the crest as it does, permitted me to take what comfort I could from the warm northerly fair weather breezes that prevailed. Indeed, most of

A stand of flowering Natal redtop grass (Rhynchelytrum repens) *– a pioneer grass that flourishes on disturbed land and is often an indicator that overgrazing has taken place.*

The least tractable of all bovines, the buffalo exerts a fascination that flows from its great strength and shy savage ways.

the rhinos in the district had moved up for the same reason and I carefully skirted downwind, passing unnoticed.

I stared about me. I was new to Umfolozi and this walk was a reconnoitre to get the feel of the country. The terrain is for the most part gently undulating, with sudden steep hills based on sandstone or dolerite formations; wooded grasslands or savannas with acacias predominate.

There came an aroma, feral and seductive, that I was never to identify. No matter – I have made a small study of things African but there is so much left to know that one more mystery is less frustrating than beguiling.

Bellows and the crash of heavy bodies alerted me to the presence of buffalo ahead. I drew nearer, moving carefully, but so preoccupied were they with their own affairs that my caution seemed hardly necessary. There was much lowing and blowing and intimidating growls; the clatter of hoof on stone and the hefty thumps of colliding meat and bone as bulls confronted each other or chased after reluctant cows. And then I sat, not uncomfortably, in the fork of a twisted *Acacia nilotica*, on a sunleached March morning on Msaseneni ridge, amongst them.

These wild cattle exert a powerful aura of fascination that flows from their great strength and shy savage ways. They are surely the least tractable of all bovines and have seldom been domesticated to serve man. It is this quality of uncompromising wildness that accounts

for the air of threat and enigma that clings to them.

The old bulls were solid black and immensely heavy through the body, their hides, worn threadbare and shiny in places, were packed with dried mud, blistered and flaking. Tattered ears and long-tassled tails were forever moving, keeping the flies on the rise. Low-slung testicles; manure-spattered rumps; horns broad and pitted across the boss, polished smooth and purposeful where they swept down then up to points that flashed sharp glints of warning. As they bulked through the herd the subordinate bulls watched them warily, ready to move aside.

The calves ranged in colour from tan to brick red. Their mournful bawling evoked memories of a cowshed at milking time, as did the dark brown barnyard smell of the heaving herd. I know the smell well.

Redbilled oxpeckers patrolled the backs and flanks of the herd and hung from their heads with insolent familiarity. The buffalo were totally oblivious to my proximity and the birds – incorrigible informers – seemed unable to recognize a human in a tree. Several buffalo passed close enough to permit the flies on their flanks to cross over to me. I submitted to their swarming persistence without trying to ward them off – a sudden movement might be noticed. Anyway it was a small enough price to pay for the privilege of being there. As the herd moved on I tried to imprint on my

memory the quality of that moment – the heat, the flies, milling beasts and raised dust, the primeval splendour of it all. There was nowhere else in the world I would rather have been at that moment.

My camp was a pitched tent around which heavy cable had been strung to keep rhinos out. The precaution was a necessary one as rhinos have a penchant for experimentally stabbing at anything man-made or bearing human scent. Water tanks get holed, signposts uprooted, fences unstrung and raingauges prodded out of shape. One of the early residents at the cottage alongside which I had camped woke one night to find his makeshift wire-enclosed verandah being demolished by a rhino using one of the uprights as a rubbing post.

The cottage – a ramshackle affair – was referred to as the Thobothi outpost. Its occupants were two British postgraduates doing research work in Umfolozi. Richard Emslie, from Cambridge, is a hard-working, hard-talking, marginally demented Scottish extrovert. He is also an amateur hypnotist – and will help cure your smoking habit 'if you have absolutely made up your mind you want to quit.' Brian O'Regan is the other half of what Umfolozi personnel had taken to calling the terrible twins. He is researching the browsing dynamics of Umfolozi's ungulates that will earn him his PhD from Oxford. He is a man of many talents and well travelled. Brian is quiet, introspective and intellectual, with a personality totally at odds with that of his companion in isolation. It was remarkable how well they got along.

Richard's study involves the grazing impact of wild herbivores, particularly white rhino, on their Umfolozi habitat. With the prospect of another drought the subject seemed especially relevant.

In the light of developing ideas on plant-herbivore relationships it has become clear that the key to Umfolozi's conservation lies in the correct management of its grass communities. Perennial grasslands have shrunk markedly over the years, reducing the white rhino's dry season emergency food reserves. Over the two drought years of 1979 and 1980 immature white rhino mortalities increased by 800 per cent. Waterbuck, and common and mountain reedbuck which use tall grass to hide from predators all suffered heavy population declines during this period.

It has become apparent that to conserve the grasslands, herbivores must be correctly managed. By judiciously controlling their numbers with removal programmes, optimum defoliation levels can be achieved. If not, irreparable habitat damage and a future long-term reduction in the park's carrying capacity are distinct possibilities.

The white rhino exerts a greater impact on the grasslands than any other herbivore. It has a relatively inefficient digestive system and consequently a huge daily food intake. According to a 1978 helicopter census they formed about 45 per cent of the pure grazing biomass. Even after the removal of 500 – nearly half the resident population – they still account for 35 per cent. The animals captured for translocation in 1980 were in such poor condition that only half the normal drug dosage was required to immobilize them. The situation has been termed the 'white rhino problem' by some ecologists and is in many ways similar to the elephant overpopulation problems occurring throughout Africa although possibly even more serious because the soil itself is being damaged.

Thobothi has its own neighbourly white rhinos. There is a broken-horned, well-mannered old territorial bull named John Lunn by the boys after a rather uncompromising fullback who played for Dunfermane Athletic Football Club's

'68 cup-winning side. It was agreed that an uncompromising attitude is essential in a fullback and a rhino bull if he is to successfully defend his territory. There is also a subordinate bull named Harry Melrose after an inside-forward, but it was never made clear whether the rhino's social inferiority was a comment on his namesake's standard of play.

In Umfolozi where the sun rises high my day always started early. Having walked for two hours on one particular day it was still only 8 am and already the heat was formidable. My wanderings had taken me to Ukhukho Ridge hard against the western boundary. The country was unlike any other I had come across in Zululand but hauntingly reminiscent of Namibia's sere bruised landscapes: avocado-green trees and silver grass contrasting starkly against patches of red earth; ancient tumbled boulders; zebra and wildebeest in ones and twos, as if the land was too poor to support herds; fleeting, soil-red impala; blue

waxbills and dueting shrikes; the white calcified pelvic girdle of a long-dead giraffe – all as I had remembered it.

This was Africa at its truest, in its basic form, lean and tough, unencumbered by adornments. It was here that a confrontation took place in 1961 between a detachment of Natal Parks rangers and a Zulu impi of 150 men who insisted on their right to hunt. There was no fence in those days separating tribal lands from the park and the Zulus were contesting the Parks Board's legality in administering Ukhukho. They claimed the land and its wildlife to be theirs; and brought the issue to a head. They and their dogs had decimated a herd of some 30 mountain reedbuck before the rangers could bring in reinforcements. It was a tense situation with advances and retreats on both sides. Indeed, not until the leaders of the opposing forces put aside their firearms and came forward to parley was it resolved, and then only temporarily. The Zulus withdrew with-

out there being any casualties but it was a close thing. Two years later the army moved Chief Zungu and his people off Ukhukho to a site west of the park. It is still quite common in these parts to find shattered grindstones left behind in accordance with Zulu tradition when a kraal is abandoned, voluntarily or not.

Umfolozi is resonant with volatile history; it permeates the atmosphere. Geologically it represents a thousand million years of time, from the very birth of life on earth. Most of its prehistory is lost however and will probably never be unravelled. The first humans to have lived there did so a lot earlier than the first date of which there is firm evidence. Polychrome paintings in Hluhluwe and Umfolozi testify to the existence of Khoisan bushmen who may have survived in the area as late as the 18th century. They were then either absorbed into the Nguni society that had occupied the coastal areas from the 4th century AD, or were driven westwards into the Drakensberg by the

increasing competition for space. What-ever their fate – death, dispersion or ab-sorption – it sought them out almost everywhere they existed.

The little aboriginal hunter-gatherers thought of themselves as the 'people of the early race'. They were the first to come and the first to go, leaving little evidence of their passage; their most poi-gnant relics being the examples of rock art scattered throughout the country.

A game scout had been detailed to lead me to Nqabaneni Hill where Umfo-lozi's best preserved painting was to be found. His name was Khishwanqani Hlatshwayo – a pleasant shy man who spoke no English – old enough to have had his earlobes pierced yet not so old as to have stretched them to accommodate plugs. Before setting out he unself-consciously cleaned his nostrils in the old manner, by pinching the bridge of his nose between thumb and middle fin-ger and blowing hard.

The climb up Nqabaneni was a stiff

The confluence of the Black and White Umfolozi rivers was used as a natural trap by the Zulu king Chaka in the great hunt of 1819. Khishwanqani indicates one of the few surviving relics of Khoisan bushmen occupancy of these parts.
In western Umfolozi one still finds shattered grindstones left behind whenever a kraal was abandoned.

Umfolozi's wooded savannas are rich in birds – hadeda ibis (below) greet each new day with raucous brays; a redbilled hornbill fastidiously grooms itself; flowering aloes tempt a glossy starling to probe for sweet nectar; a martial eagle stands guard over its monitor lizard kill warily eyeing another eagle circling overhead; reacting nervously to a rustle in the grass, a crested francolin peers about anxiously.

one and we were both sweating freely by the time we reached the summit. Even there, on this precipice-defended plateau was a rhino's dunging midden. We scrambled down a sheer face between lichen decorated rocks, clutching at rock figs for balance. Then, on a narrow ledge the game scout stopped and pointed, 'Mphofu,' he said – eland. And there inscribed in ochre at the back of a cave was the unmistakeable image of an eland, heavy-humped and fecund-looking.

The Khoisan held the eland in almost mystic regard. In their folklore they describe its relationship to Mantis (the praying mantis to which they attributed divine powers): 'The Eland was the one to whom the Mantis once gave some wasp's honey; this is why he is dark, because he once ate wasp's honey. The Hartebeest and the Eland are things of the Mantis; therefore they have magic power. People say that the Mantis first made the Eland; the Hartebeest was the one whom he made after the death of his Eland. That is why he did not love the Eland and the Hartebeest only a little, he loved them dearly, for he made his heart

of the Eland and the Hartebeest.' Like the Khoisan, the eland too, has disappeared from these parts.

We moved on to a larger cave but lacking suitable surfaces it had no art. The ceiling, honeycombed by water erosion, was blackened in places by past camp fires. There were, too, the shattered remains of adobe nests, abandoned by wasps and swallows, clinging to the ceiling. In the loose shale of the cave's floor was the hoof imprint of a small antelope, presumably a klipspringer. A rock pigeon had winged hurriedly away on our arrival and a pervasive strong stink indicated baboons had used the cave to sleep in at night. Below, the brown White Umfolozi River executed a curve. A file of nyala appeared from a plumed stand of phragmites, forded the shallow river and disappeared into the forest on the opposite bank. I looked out over a faded landscape of worn-out browns and greys without road or scar or any sign that technological man had been there – a Khoisan world.

I have met several people who claim the dubious distinction of rounding up

the last of Etosha's 'wild' Khoisan. Their rationale is that they were interfering with the environment. What they failed to understand is that the Khoisan were the environment, or at least an intrinsic part of it.

That airy, former Khoisan castle – now their cenotaph – also rings with ancient Zulu history. Nqabaneni means the 'Hill of Refusal' in Zulu and takes its name from a battle waged between Chaka's Zulus and Chief Zwide's Ndwandwes who inhabited all the country to the west of the Mpila Hills. It was in the early years of Chaka's ascendency and the battle was a crucial one as Zwide was his most serious rival. Zwide occupied the heights so in the interests of a more equitable fight Chaka invited him to come down and engage his army on the plains. Zwide wisely refused, he nqaba-ed, so Chaka resorted to a brilliant stratagem.

He first sent a detachment of warriors to skirmish the enemy on the hill's more gradual ascent to divert their attention while a squad of hand-picked men scaled the cliffs on the other side in what must

have been Zululand's first ever commando raid. The tactic worked perfectly and the Ndwandwes, attacked from behind as well as the front, were overrun. Eventually this whole area was annexed by Chaka and designated a Royal hunting preserve.

My days had by now settled into a regular pattern. Each morning after sunrise and a cup of coffee I set off carrying a camera satchel with a small assortment of lenses and spare film; a pair of binoculars; a waterbottle, its contents heavily laced with an orange isotonic mix, and a tripod slung across my shoulders. With time I reduced my hiking outfit to black PT shorts and a pair of boots worn without socks. Socks only attract ticks so I dispensed with them after two days, but not before raising a rash of bites around my ankles.

Ticks are Zululand's universal curse. Nymphs, about the size of a pinhead and referred to as pepper ticks, are the worst. Often the effects of their bites are only felt days later, when the itch is excruciating. With a problem so uncomfortable and extensive, ideas for beating

the little pests naturally proliferate. They range from prevention – stand over a smokey fire before going walking, or wear canine flea collars around your ankles – to cure – add ammonia to your bathwater after a walk. Do not scratch tick bites as this only releases histamines that aggravate. But the relief a good scratch provides usually means this last warning goes unheeded. Even if one resists the temptation by day one ends up clawing away while asleep.

As was to be expected I eventually contracted tickbite fever. I count myself lucky that it was only a mild dose which nevertheless provided me with a measure of immunity against recurrent bouts. I also came down with a severe case of malaria which meant five days in hospital with hot and cold shivers, racking headaches and nausea. But for anyone intending to spend any length of time in sub-tropical wild places such maladies are really no more than rites of passage. More grievous was the cholera that raged throughout the tribal districts, spread far and wide by polluted streams and rivers on which the rural Zulus depend for drinking and washing.

My camp at Thobothi had assumed an air of rooted permanence. Native creepers had clamped tendrils on the tent's uprights and guyropes. Striped skinks had invested the tent, establishing canvas territories which they defended with the quick push-ups thought to be territorial threat displays. They also waged welcome war on invading flies.

The collection of lizards was more than welcome but unfortunately they attracted the attention of a spotted bush snake, which had entered the tent on hunting forays. Although non-venomous I found myself unable to tolerate its comings and goings. When it next arrived I tugged on its tail and generally made it feel unwanted, hoping it would get the message and stay away – it did.

The local wagtails and thrushes were fascinated by my Kombi's side mirror and gathered to combat their reflections with fierce, outraged pecks. A flock of redbilled oxpeckers had roosted in a tall acacia overhanging the cottage and every time they saw us they hissed their alarm call, never becoming habituated, although by now they must have realized

we meant them no harm. A pair of lilac-breasted rollers scorched the air above my tent with extraordinary tumbling aerial displays accompanied by raucous screeches when other birds ventured too near their haunts. In flight the handsomely coloured rollers reflected the sun, spinning turquoise lights in the parched air. And each evening there was a harmony of dove calls as various species competed for the listener's attention. The harsh cooing of Cape turtle doves, offset by the monotonous chant of the emerald-spotted wood dove, the two shot through by that most characteristic sound of Africa, the 'Coo-coo-cook-KOO-kuk-coo' of the redeyed turtle dove.

Thobothi is on high ground just before it slopes to the Black Umfolozi River which here serves as Umfolozi's western boundary – beyond is KwaZulu tribal homelands.

Over weekends, from the kraal across the river, on the wind came the thump of a much-loved cowhide drum, reverberating throughout the night until the early hours of the morning. Contrary to popular misconception there is nothing sinister or ominous about the persistent, rhythmic pounding. It simply means that all is well in the land, that there is a dance or beer-drink in the village this night. I have lain awake in my tent in the dark and heard the drumbeats overlaid by the roar of a restless lion and thought that I should never hear a more noble sound or one that so utterly concentrates the attention.

During our stay in Umfolozi we lived close to nature. While bathing in the sycamore fig-lined rivers it was not unusual to see big game such as this lioness crossing upstream. As long as we kept silent and moved slowly animals went on their way without fear or threat.

Each golden pre-dawn, flights of hadeda ibises en route from their roosts to upriver feeding grounds announced the day with discordant startling brays. There came too a volley of cock crows; the whistles and shouts of herdboys mustering cattle and the hysterical barking of lean yellow pi-dogs; resonant peasant voices carried in the still air and laughter chimed fat and uninhibited. I know I am in Africa when I awake to these sounds, they have an atavistic familiarity that is deeply reassuring.

Inside the Thobothi cottage during the daylight hours was the soft creaking of woodborers eating the house down around our ears. All the wooden figurines purchased from young Zulu roadside carvers were pierced by neat symmetrical holes, sunk clean as if by precision tools. By night field mice were abroad, swopping shopping hints as to the most accessible fruit, vegetable and grain caches. Cockroaches swarmed, sugar ants overran and termites invisibly undermined. Geckoes and spiders, our only allies, were few, choosy and easily surfeited.

Rather than despair we learned to accept that firstly, nothing is permanent, sacrosanct or wholly owned, and secondly, they probably need it more than we do.

The first is an African concept, born of time spent sharing a continent with age-old indominatable forces that have grudgingly been inculcated into a mainstream that simply aspires to persist. The second is a European sophistry – having conquered Nature, we now try to appease her. This reaction can only be arrived at once basic comforts have been secured. It is an aesthetic consideration

Wielding their massive heads like sledgehammers, two giraffe bulls engage in a spectacular 'necking' fight.
When a strike connects the sound of impact can be heard up to 100 metres away.

Sparring impala rams push and twist in an effort to unbalance the opponent and so permit a thrust with rapier-sharp horns.

In summer, during the breeding season, the male tree agama changes its cryptic grey coloration for this handsome display, the better to attract females. Nonchalantly defying gravity, he clings to the woodborer-scarred trunk of a dead acacia.

and as such is amicable to and out of sympathy with the African's struggle for survival. For all the advances, life in a tribal village remains a precarious business, where malnutrition and infectious diseases are a daily fact of life. Fundamental political and human rights together with freedom from hunger and deprivation must be attained before subsistence societies can be rallied to the cause of conservation.

There, at Thobothi, all the ingredients came together: the villagers scrabbling to make a living against increasing odds; the wildlife and circumscribed ecosystems crowding to the edge of survival; scientists unlocking nature's secrets at the same time as their study subject reels before unprecedented onslaughts while the reporter records and clarifies the issues so that none can say 'we didn't know'.

Four o'clock one dark morning, with a light drizzle falling, a small pride of lions chased and caught a zebra foal just outside my tent. The drumming of the pursued zebra's hooves woke me and I was fully alert when it was seized. The foal's sharp high-pitched distress whinny sounded just like an oestrus mare rejecting a stallion's advances and at first I thought that was what I was hearing. Nearby a white rhino huffed in agitation followed almost immediately by the growls and rumblings of lions disputing a kill. I lay for nearly two hours listening to their wrangling and the breaking of bones until almost dawn when it became quiet except for the repeated rallying calls of the foal's mother.

At first light I was out to investigate but the lions had gone. The episode had taken place only 50 metres from my tent yet I found no sign of the little that remained and had begun doubting what I had heard until a scavenging crow led me to the spot.

The carcass had been torn apart by what appeared, judging from the areas of impacted red earth, to have been three lions, each eventually going off by itself with what it had salvaged, to eat in peace. All that remained as testimony to the night's minor drama were two bloodied fetlocks, a shattered skull, strewn bones and a heap of grey, hair-spiked lion dung. The mare continued circling right up until mid-morning, crying out

all the while, finally giving up only when the departing herd called her away.

Lions were formerly widespread and quite common in Zululand but with the advance of progress their numbers inevitably dwindled until they disappeared altogether from Umfolozi in 1938. Thereafter the only hold-outs were to be found east of the Lebombo mountains in the vicinity of Mkuzi Game Reserve, and in Tongaland, but they too were destroyed during the Second World War. Then in 1958 a lone black-maned male turned up in Umfolozi from Moçambique, having frustrated the best efforts of irate ranchers, on whose cattle he had preyed, to

shoot him. In 1965 several lionesses were introduced and the population soon expanded. One consequence was that young males evicted from the pride tended to stray beyond the park's boundaries, rustling cattle and posing a threat to human life in the densely inhabited tribal lands. There was no alternative and it is now policy to routinely cull all young lions found along the boundary fence and to immediately follow-up and destroy any that break out.

On my first walk I came across a pride of nine lions – all lionesses and young adults. I saw them from the northern summit of Mbulunga Ridge as they sprawled on an outcrop below, unaware of my arrival. Three adolescent males, their soft manes newly erupting, had climbed onto the confined space of an umbrella thorn, piling on top of each other in an effort to settle. A lioness stared up at where I sat in full view, unable to make me out but vaguely suspicious nevertheless. Her tail twitched apprehensively but when I remained still she seemed reassured and flopped down in the shade, sitting up every so often to reaffirm that all was well.

Finally the pride stirred themselves, stiffly rising to indulge in sensual stretching and cavernous yawns, the young males coming down from the tree in an awkward flurry of clutchings and scrabblings to land heavily. Led by an old female they started in single file up a gametrail that led directly to where I sat. I thought it not a good idea to let them get any closer so I suddenly stood up and they froze in their tracks. They glared at me for a moment, intensely appraising the situation, ears cocked, alert and tense expressions on their faces then they turned in concert and bolted at a crouching trot, glancing back over their shoulders in alarm.

Strange to say I never encountered lions in that area again. The first pride had obviously been nomadic and simply moved on but in spite of the many zebra and wildebeest grazing the Gqoyini bottomlands no resident pride operated there during my stay. Umfolozi's territorial prides concentrate their activities along the riverbanks where herbivores are abundant and reedbeds and thickets provide excellent stalking cover. For that reason I avoided the rivers when on

A white-browed coucal ruffles its rain-soaked feathers towards the sun that has re-appeared in the wake of a brief shower. Its rapid liquid song is said to presage rain.

It is in the rainy summer months when the land is at its most nutritious that Umfolozi's herbivores give birth. Warthog piglets are born into a world full of dangers and within the first six months half of the usual litter of four to five may be lost, although this family has survived intact.

Umfolozi giraffes show no definite seasonality in breeding and although there is a calving peak in early summer, young are also born in winter.

Impala ewes have one fawn annually. In Umfolozi the births are highly synchronized – nearly all the young are dropped in the latter half of November. Within the herd fawns form crèche groups that move and act as a unit but if danger threatens the females rush to the crèche, calling to their own offspring.

foot. I had no wish to stumble over a sleeping lion – they are one species I much prefer to observe from the shelter of a car.

In my walks I often covered ground that I had visited before and always thrilled to find my old footprints overlaid by the spoor of hyena or impala or obliterated by the three-toed, crinkly pad of a rhino. Once, in the loose, washed sand of the Thobothi stream bed my track was neatly enclosed, as if in parenthesis, by those of a passing leopard.

The next morning a cool southerly was blowing, first portent of coming rain and all the oxpeckers had taken shelter on the leeward side of the giraffes they were attending. I had followed my customary route along Msaseneni crest but that day the wind blew against me and carried my scent to a lone buffalo cow. The ominous warning sent her crashing away down the slope when suddenly she stopped, turned and came rushing back towards me. Completely taken aback and thinking perhaps she was one of the villainous man-hunters I had heard of, I scrambled into a tree. But she stopped well short of me and peering into a sward of long grass, encouraged a still wet, black, trembling calf to its feet then hurriedly led it away. They fled across the open grasslands without breaking stride until they reached a fold in the land, a drainage line, where rain run-off had given rise to dense enveloping riparian forest. At the edge of the treeline the cow pulled up and swivelled to stare long and hard at where I stood, silhouetted on the ridge, then reassuringly nuzzling her calf she slipped from sight into the safety of the dark undergrowth.

The weather had finally turned. Humidity had risen dramatically and the dark blue sky to the south looked cool and moist. Back at Thobothi that evening I asked Joseph, Brian O'Regan's assistant, if he predicted rain but he con-

Through the viewfinder the leopard's impenetrable yellow gaze met and locked with mine. I fired the shutter but the alien metallic sound was more than she could bear. With a harsh, rasping growl she bounded away, leaving a trembling in the air from the tension of her passage.

No sooner had the sun set than these cheetahs, three young brothers, roused themselves from beneath an umbrella thorn where they had lounged all afternoon and set off under a full moon to hunt in the Gqoyini Valley.

fidently shook his head. That night the sky opened and sheets of water fell as hard as rain can come.

We needed the rain, God knows, but I wasn't prepared for that. Too many cosy campsites under spreading acacias had perforated the tent's canopy with a plethora of thornpricks. My shelter from the storm leaked like a sieve. The uninspired pass I had made around the tent's perimeter in an unconvincing imitation of a stormwater trench-cum-exclusion wall proved inadequate within minutes. The torrent filled up the ditch, percolated through the dyke, eddied

across the groundsheet and I was awash. The rising tide marked its progress with a dark highwater line on my foamrubber mattress, which stood at groundlevel. I circled, seeking a dry corner, reluctant to admit defeat. Ten minutes later I gave up. Grabbing my camera cases I dashed for the cottage. My noisy arrival through the hinged screen door marginally roused Richard and he sleepily mumbled from the comfort of his bunk 'Still raining?' I didn't answer. If he didn't know it was still raining he wouldn't have missed my reply. That man would sleep through Armageddon.

I towelled my head dry, then settled down under homemade posters that urged 'Reunite Gondwanaland!' and, with jingoist enthusiasm, 'Keep the Falklands British!' and felt fortified by a mug of instant black coffee primed with an unmeasured tot of good Scotch. Under the harsh light of a gas lantern I settled to reread Joseph Conrad's excellent 'Heart of Darkness' – a reminder that things can be a lot worse. It was a long night but at least warm and dry – not comforts to be taken lightly after my previous situation.

Francolins greeted a shrouded dawn with wild racketing. I read – 'The offing was barred by a black bank of cinuds, and the tranquil waterway leading to the uttermost ends of the earth flowed sombre under an overcast sky – seemed to lead into the heart of an immense dark-

Climbing and resting in trees is popular among the younger lions of Umfolozi . . . but they look clumsy and lack the assurance and sinuous grace of a leopard.

ness' – then closed the book and stepped outside. Yesterday's dustbowl had become a swamp. Rainwater was not merely in puddles but in a single unbroken sheet. Overwhelmed by dark burly clouds the day broke dour and inconclusive.

The transition from night into day, usually so abrupt in the sub-tropics, was signalled more by the unholy clamouring of hadeda hordes than by any improvement in illumination. Certainly the skinks, whose day is governed by the warmth of the sun, recognized no shift – they stayed out of sight. They depend on the sun's rays to thaw them and are at a severe disadvantage in the open on cool mornings – too chilled to hurry out of harm's way if the necessity arises.

A whitebrowed coucal ruffled out its feathers and meticulously preened itself dry. It may have had forewarning of its soaking – I had heard the descending liquid notes of its song the whole of the previous day and its call is said to presage rain.

The birds were marvellous – they whistled, croaked, chirruped and got moving regardless of the conditions.

They have high metabolic rates that must be serviced and cannot afford delay. For the insectivores the rains had opened a treasure chest of invertebrates stimulated by the precipitation to come out of hiding. The yellowbilled kites that had not yet departed to their northern retreats swooped on ascending winged termite nymphs, plucked them out of the air with their talons and transferred them to their bills without missing a beat. And as always when the coming of the rains ends a dry spell, up comes the beautiful smell of grateful earth.

After the initial cloudburst rain continued to fall in a productive cycle of showers followed by sunshine. The summer drought had been broken. Until then Umfolozi had braced itself for another bitter winter but was quick to take advantage of its good fortune and the land recovered miraculously. New growth sparkled green, with flowers everywhere. Burgeoning mushroom heads and colourful wild fruit appeared overnight. On the hillslopes tall stands of *Themeda* waved in the moist breezes like fields of ripe wheat. The haze that had

overhung everything was gone and distant dark-rumpled blue hills stood in sharp relief against a wash of electric blue sky. The earth exhaled a new fragrance carried by fresh southerlies – promise of more rain to come.

In view of the importance of the late rains I tried to be gracious in the face of a massive increase in ticks and flies but cursing, scratching and slapping, I found it not always easy. It served to highlight my conviction that to appreciate wild Africa one must experience it at close quarters. Without the bites and thorns its true nature goes unrealized.

The spectre of drought was only one of many threats Umfolozi had faced since its inception. Its checkered history reflected regular and precarious swings between disaster and survival. In 1915 a deputation of angry farmers forced the Provincial Administration to deproclaim 23 000 ha of the reserve and so began a controversy that was to menace Umfolozi's existence for years to come.

Centre stage was the tsetse, a rubbery flat fly of the genus *Glossina* which transmits trypanosomiasis – nagana – to do-

Nature has taken its course.

mestic stock although wildlife lives in balance with it and breaks down to disease only under stress. At the turn of the century the two Umfolozi rivers and the Hluhluwe and Mkuzi rivers were infested with tsetse. When in 1918 farms south of Umfolozi were opened up as land grants to ex-servicemen a clash between the interests of European progress and wildlife became inevitable. A great deal of agitation arose for the destruction of wild ungulates accused of acting as reservoirs for the disease. Accordingly a series of game eradication campaigns were instigated with the intention of eliminating the fly by removing its food source.

In 1922 an unspecified number of animals were shot and the onslaught was renewed in 1929. The object this time was to remove the teeming herds occupying the statelands surrounding Umfolozi and create a *cordon sanitaire* between the reserve and the ranches. In a legalized massacre lasting 18 months 32 684 head of game were recorded as being shot, a minimum figure that does not take into

account the large numbers which must have been wounded and not tallied.

Between 1930 and 1939 there was a lull in the incidence of nagana and the killing was suspended but in 1939 new outbreaks prompted demands that game elimination be extended to cover all of tsetse-infested Zululand except Hluhluwe Game Reserve. Hunters invaded Umfolozi's sanctuary with instructions to shoot everything except rhinos.

Shooting commenced in Umfolozi in December 1942, initially on a small scale, as it was feared that a direct and immediate all out assault on western Umfolozi's high density areas might disperse game and possibly tsetse into neighbouring tribal lands and farming settlements. The idea was to encroach gradually, from the periphery towards the large concentrations. Hunters collected the tails of animals shot and expended cartridges had to be accounted for. The standard of shooting was high, a little over two rounds per carcass. Such efficiency resulted in the deaths of

70 332 animals before the programme was terminated in 1950 by which time zebra, wildebeest and impala had been totally exterminated from Umfolozi and kudu, waterbuck and buffalo were greatly reduced.

And still the fly persisted. Killing over 100 000 head of game wasn't enough; it resulted only in wholesale waste and appalling destruction. The tsetse was eventually wiped out by the aerial spraying of pesticides. In 1952 when Umfolozi was handed back to the Natal Parks Board game was so scarce that patrolling rangers doffed their hats to any animal encountered – a mark of respect for its sagacity in surviving the holocaust.

Umfolozi's recovery started at once. Buffalo, wildebeest and zebra migrated south from Hluhluwe and multiplied. As did impala and nyala. One advantage of the slaughter was that white rhinos were able to increase without competition from other grazers and prolific breeders such as warthog bounced back through natural increase. The terrible wounds of the ill-fated nagana campaigns healed remarkably quickly.

The good rains brought the rivers down in spate. Their torrents boiled dirty red-brown, the same colour as the land through which they passed. Indeed it is the earth's crust, its precious topsoil, that is carried along by the swollen waters on their way to the sea. My hand vanished a mere few centimetres below the murky surface. My companion, Hlatshwayo, again my guide, this time to the confluence of the two Umfolozis, shook his head in disgust. He had no water bottle but in spite of a heat that roared he declined to drink from the muddy river.

The Black Umfolozi is perennial, but in common with many other African rivers, increasing soil erosion in the catchment has meant violent summer floods and a reduced year-long flow. In July 1963 an unseasonal torrential downpour lasting for days caused flooding that completely demolished the bordering riverine forest, casting enormous sycamore figs far beyond the normal floodbanks. The heavy deposits of silt laid down during this upheaval transformed the formerly deep, swift and rocky river to its present shallow state, with its wide flat sandy beds.

The White Umfolozi had always been clear and meandering with a surface flow that persisted through most winters but nowadays only scattered pools remain during the dry season. The rivers meet on Umfolozi's north-eastern boundary where Chaka in 1819 organized a great hunt on a scale never before attempted.

It was planned as carefully as a military expedition and aimed at encircling all the game between the rivers, then driving them into the natural trap formed by the rivers' junction. Fords were heavily guarded and thorn fences forming tunnels led to deep pitfalls, disguised with wooden lattices, branches

and grass. Beyond them a light fence screened hunters positioned to attack any animal that escaped the pits. Survivors of those two assaults had finally to negotiate the steep ridge flanking the river. Elephants labouring up the declivity were set upon by axe-wielding warriors bent on hamstringing them – a particularly dangerous sport.

The pitfalls are still there and in a good state of preservation – commemorating stirring times. On the day of Chaka's hunt many elephants, buffalo and rhino were killed as were quite a few Zulu braves. Bush pigs apparently refused to be driven across the river and broke back through the line of beaters, inflicting casualties as they retreated. The fugitives ran into a rearguard of men and dogs rounding up wounded game and fierce fights broke out with old boars and sows defending their young. Lions and leopards were last to come, preceeded by jackals, wild dogs and hyenas and all were engaged with reckless enthusiasm.

As I gazed down upon the confluence from the vantage point of Siyembeni Hill where Chaka may have stood directing operations, it seemed that not much had changed except that both rivers were badly silted and easy to ford. Cliffs dominating the river's edge forced the harried elephants to resort to the few, well-reinforced game paths that existed, one of which we used to descend. At the bottom a lone buffalo with a cattle egret astride its back, drank then waded the Black Umfolozi with heavy measured tread. His head was encased by horns that swept down then tipped up, oddly reminiscent of the silly hats still worn by some ladies to English tea-parties. The old bull ignored the happy, shrill chatter of Zulu women collecting water but the commotion was sufficient to cause a basking crocodile to glide from a sandbar into the water.

I had built a hide in the shadow of a Transvaal gardenia adjacent to a large rain-filled pan in the Gqoyini catchment and spent many days and full-moon nights there, privy to the comings and goings and secret exchanges of the creatures that came to drink. The most intriguing insights were not only of high drama, although there was plenty of that, but also the continuity, the patient enduring rhythms, the daily repetition of affairs attended to without fuss or ceremony that best typified the ambience around the pan. I soon came to recognize regular visitors – the herds of wildebeest, zebra, impala and giraffe, family groups of warthogs and individual rhinos. It was the unexpected that usually provided the thrills.

One warm winter morning I was jolted out of my reverie by a kudu alarm barking. Looking about I saw with a rush of excitement a small female leopard come purposefully from a euclea thicket and, ignoring the disturbance her arrival had caused, make straight for the water. She drank nervously, stopping frequently to glance around, hindquarters braced high; the sound of her lapping carried clearly on the dry air. My hide had passed muster – the leopard looked at it and through it without a hint of suspicion. Finished drinking she walked up a shallow gulley that channelled rain run-off into the pan that brought her to within 20 metres of me.

The click of my camera stopped her in mid-stride. Her chin fur was darkly damp and still dripping from her drink; her tail lashed distractedly, the tip rakishly angled where it had once been broken. Through the viewfinder her impenetrable yellow gaze met and locked with mine. I fired the shutter again but the alien sound was more than she could bear. With a harsh, rasping growl she bounded away, leaving a trembling in the air from the tension of her passage.

Unlike the secretive, nocturnal leopard which was, to a remarkable degree, able to adapt to and co-exist with civilization's advance, the cheetah retreated in lockstep with the shrinking edges of wilderness. It was seen no more in Umfolozi after the 1920s and the last sighting in Zululand was near Bube Pan in Mkuzi Game Reserve in 1941. Beginning in 1965 however, a re-introduction programme has been in effect and a nucleus has settled down and bred.

I encountered cheetah fairly regularly in my wanderings. A lone animal roamed in the vicinity of Thobothi and we were occasionally alerted to its presence by a fusillade of impala warning snorts. In Gqoyini lived another loner that I periodically came across, once on a nyala fawn kill, but it remained extremely shy and unapproachable. On the other hand three young brothers that also occupied Gqoyini would permit me a careful approach by car to within some 35 metres but would bolt immediately at the sight of a human on foot.

Because of the wooded, broken nature of the country I was unable to follow cheetah as they went about their business as I had done in Etosha. The best I managed was to spend a day in the brothers' company as they lounged beneath an umbrella thorn, moving only to realign themselves with the shifting shade. A pale full moon hung in the afternoon sky and I guessed the cheetahs would wait till nightfall before setting out to hunt.

A cluster of giraffe, overcome by their innate curiosity, edged up to the sprawled cheetahs. A young cow, drawn irresistibly nearer, raised and lowered her head then leaned from left to right – utterly mesmerized – viewing the source of her wonder from every angle. That she recognized them as predators was apparent from her occasional exhala-

tions, like gruff sighs, that pass as alarm calls amongst giraffe.

As I had predicted no sooner had the sun set than the cheetahs roused themselves and moved off, scattering the startled giraffe into a rocking retreat. The lithe cats were quickly swallowed up in the undergrowth and gathering gloom. I was left feeling frustrated that after my vigil I would miss out on the action to come. Instead of going home I decided to put in a few hours at the hide, little guessing how dramatically the day's inactivity could be compensated.

The pan by night bears no resemblance to its appearance by day. A huge moon radiated transparent silver light and broken spectral trees cast long dense shadows. The melodious quaver of a fierynecked nightjar, the litany bird, beseeched 'Good Lord deliver us,' over and over again. A hyena whooped from close at hand, with a distinctive break at the top of its scale. A shifty jackal trotted in its hangdog way to the water, pulled up suddenly, thought better of it and went back into the night. A tree frog throbbed sonorously.

There was a clatter of hooves and a kudu cow cantered down to the pan's

Kudu are common in Umfolozi, preferring lightly-bushed areas and savanna, only entering thicker bush during the heat of the day.

Dawn is announced by the deep booming calls of ground hornbills; although both sexes boom they differ in tone. So distinctive is the sound that it has caught the local people's imagination: 'I'm going, I'm going, I'm going home to my relations!' and the male replies 'You can go, you can go, you can go home to your relations!'

edge. She was, mysteriously, alone – kudus are gregarious by nature. She didn't pause to drink, just threw a glance back over her shoulder and hurriedly panicked on. Moments later a pair of hyenas shuffled in from the dark. They were not running but moved with an air of determination that was taut with menace. I suspected they were on the kudu's trail. Without breaking stride they went off in her direction.

I was wondering what the outcome would be when the kudu suddenly reappeared, running hard now, with the hyenas coursing her not far behind. She splashed into the water, hesitated a moment, then galloped on, while the hyenas, with a single-mindedness born of confidence, doggedly held to her spoor. Once again they disappeared but not for long. In desperation the kudu apparently believed the shallow pan offered a last hope of sanctuary and returned a third time, the hyenas still in close attendance.

By now the kudu was plainly exhausted and in the middle of the pan she turned to face her tormentors, futilely butting at them as they circled, seeking an opening. The tension was too much and she pivoted to flee. A hyena moved to head her off, she swerved, faltered and the second hyena seized her haunch in a lockjaw.

Brought to bay in a shallow pan by a pair of spotted hyenas, an exhausted kudu cow turns to face her tormentors, and her fate. The hyenas had earlier cut her from the security of the herd and doggedly coursed her until this moment when her strength gave out. Seconds after this picture was taken she was seized in a lockjaw from behind and the chase was over. Above, a hyena waits . . .

The doomed animal no longer attempted to defend herself. As the hyenas chewed through her hide with their carnassial molars there came a breaking sound, like bones being splintered. Slowly she buckled, sinking to her brisket in the bloodied water. A giraffe came to drink, stood and stared, keeping its own counsel. Once, the kudu looked back, then groaned, a sound so shocking, so profoundly sad that I cannot forget it to this day – I doubt I ever will. Of all the kills I have witnessed – and there have been many – this was the hardest; its taking too long. Finally, mercifully, her head went down and she collapsed

on her side. The hyenas had not touched a vital organ, the kudu had simply had enough and died of shock.

It is the inconsistencies that abound in nature's majestic order that make it so fascinating. The next day, still restless, with the poignant memories of the night before I passed up the hide and went for a long walk.

The countryside swarmed with life. Kurrichane buttonquails exploded underfoot to settle again almost immediately. A mob of redbilled hoopoes scuttled up tree trunks and along branches, probing with delicate curved bills for millipedes and beetles, racket-

ing furiously while they worked. A leopard tortoise, plodding endless paths, tucked away its head as I passed. Pairs of gaudy-painted locusts, mounted in grave copulation, watch me boggle-eyed. A bateleur, reduced to a black dot and identifiable only by its cursory tail, swirled overhead; an heraldic rhino, set against the skyline stood in dark relief.

The sun burned like a flame and a hot wind slapped my face. Since the rains my walks were planned so that the midday break coincided with my arrival at a pool in the sandy bed of the Gqoyini watercourse. The brown opaque water was wonderfully refreshing and I lay with my head propped against a rock, content as a warthog in a wallow.

I shared the pool with several terrapins, an assortment of water spiders and skimmers and a young monitor lizard. The monitor's prettily patterned green and gold head broke the surface with the forthrightness of a submarine's periscope. It regarded me obliquely with suspicious stony eyes, its forked tongue flickering, looking for all the world like a miniature sea-serpent.

Birds and butterflies seeking water came and went on the scorched winds. Wasps and bees probed the mud, leaving hieroglyphic tracks. But as the heat mounted all activity gradually wound down. The noon stillness appeared complete when it was pierced by the bittersweet lament of an emeraldspotted wood dove:

> *'My father is dead*
> *And I was not told*
> *My mother is dead*
> *And I was not told*
> *My heart in pain*
> *Cries*
> *To*
> *Toto*
> *To to to to'*

Then it too fell silent.

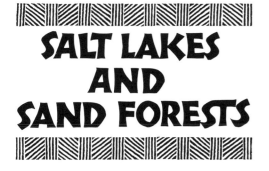

SALT LAKES AND SAND FORESTS

Vapourish clouds overhung the sky that late summer when Margot and I visited St Lucia. The humidity was intense, it seeped in everywhere and driving the well-maintained gravel road from Hluhluwe village we both longed for shorefront breezes.

We were on our way to False Bay Park which lies between the Hluhluwe and Mzinene rivers, part of the great St Lucia lake complex. False Bay itself forms the north-western arm of the H-shaped lake and the 2 274-hectare park lies on its western shoreline. The road wound through fields of pineapples topped by half-ripe fruit and past one-roomed trading stores with their weathered signs advertising a life style far removed from the one I had so recently left behind.

At the False Bay entrance gate a game-scout in soft bush hat, khaki shirt and shorts, puttees and polished boots snapped to attention and addressed us with a crackling salute. This is the standard reception at all game reserves under Natal Parks' jurisdiction. Not only does it create a good impression but the Zulu scouts seem to enjoy the martial formalities as much as the visitors do. I entered our particulars into the arrivals book and read in the permit handed me that 'because of the genuine danger from crocodiles, no swimming is allowed in the lake'.

Once in the park, dense forest crowded to the edge of the road. Amongst the thronging vegetation I recognized the smooth grey convoluted trunk of the torchwood (*Balanites mau ghamii*) – its yellowish fruit, resembling large dates, gives off a toxic substance in water and is used by tribes people as a fish poison. A family group of nyala broke cover and cantered across the road, disappearing into the bush on the other side with hardly a glance in our direction. A yellowbellied bulbul skulked unseen within the foliage, its presence revealed only by a high-pitched nasal laugh that was echoed by a neighbour.

The forest abruptly gave way to the narrow margin of hippo-cropped grassy foreshore that introduced the lake, choppy with wind and sparkling blue in the late afternoon light. A goliath heron, a pair of yellowbilled egrets and a single little egret patrolled the shallows, sidestepping the numerous jelly fish that bobbed on the tide like iridescent silver flotsam.

Although Lake St Lucia's water area is 26 800 hectares in extent – 60 kilometres long and 21 kilometres at its widest point – it is very shallow with an average depth of slightly less than one metre. It is fed by four main rivers, the Mkuzi, Mzinene, Nyalazi and Hluhluwe, as well as the Mkuzi swamp and a long narrow estuary that connects it to the sea. Its salinity and water levels vary, depending on the supply of fresh water from rainfall and river feeders but influence by man in the hydrology of the lake has increased the range of variation.

The combined effects of irrigation, damming and afforestation have resulted in a significant diminuation of fresh water inflow, especially during critical dry periods. At times the lake's salinity has risen from less than 35 parts of salt per 1 000 (that of seawater) to as much as 80 to 90 parts, or even 120 as occurred in the 1971 drought. Very few forms of life can survive such concentrations – anything immersed is soon encrusted with salt. Once the drought was broken salinity levels gradually decreased and ecological conditions improved but it still causes more concern to parks management than any other artificial factor.

We pitched our tent just back from the lake shore in a clearing on the forest fringe. A lone hippo, submerged except for bristly ears, protuberant eyes and nostrils, mutely watched while we worked. At sunset, on short thick legs, the old bull ponderously hauled his huge bulk ashore to stand motionless on the beach, his whiskered chin resting on the ground, as if drained by the effort or lost in deep contemplation. His flanks were puckered by old scars and recent wounds gaping pink in raw relief against the battleship grey hide. There would be no more wars in that old warrior's future – he had fought his last and lost. In defeat, he had come away from the herd to live out his days as a solitary outcast.

As last light faded into night, the fresh breeze coming off the lake seemed to revive him. Marshalling his reserves he plodded with solid assurance a familiar path to private pastures, passing from sight into the gathering dusk. Later that night I heard his turgid grunts, like the hollow laughter of a very old man nursing a bitter, personal joke. When his call went unanswered he did not repeat

The forest's gloomy floor is strewn with the abandoned shells of land snails, fallen fruit, lianas and leaves that fungi and bacteria will reduce to humus which in turn will support new life.

Eight species of epiphytic orchids occur in False Bay's arid sand forest on north-western St Lucia. Appearance apart, epiphytes are not parasitic but only use other plants as props without drawing energy from them. They take water directly from the moisture in the air through thin-walled aerial roots. The exquisite Aërangis mystacidii *is only one of these.*

it. Perhaps unaccustomed to loneliness he had learned to accept it.

The next morning he was back in the water, silhouetted black and imperturbable in the fiery track that reflected the rising sun. Fish were jumping, rippling the lake's glass smooth surface. A flock of redbilled teal whirred by overhead; from the woodlands came the sad, relentless song of a turtle dove.

That day Margot and I decided to investigate the Mpophomeni trail that winds through the surrounding dry sand forest. Strips of this strangely arid, dense and unique forest occur on low sandy ridges that run parallel to the coast. They occupy much of the Tongaland plains and reach their most southerly point at False Bay. They shelter several species that occur nowhere else, in particular the rare suni antelope, which few people have seen in the wild.

I lead the way, as much to warn of spiders and their webs – and the trail is festooned with them – as anything else. Golden orb spiders, the females as big as a woman's hand, loomed against the sky – long-limbed, venomous, trembling on breeze-ruffled webs that shimmered in the sunlight. Colourfully grotesque long-spined shield spiders looking, with their horned, red and yellow striped carapaces, weird and other-worldly, are much smaller and work closer to the ground. All webs were carefully skirted, a course of action that obviously pleased the spiders as much as it did Margot.

The small glossy antelopes known as red duiker were fairly common and scampered away at our approach, changing in colour from russet to a flash of bright chestnut as they crossed shafts of sunlight. They fled in silence except one,

which we came upon unawares, that reacted with an alarm whistle as jarring in the silent forest as metal on a lathe. Duikers are solitary or in pairs as befits a forest dweller. There are good ecological reasons for this; small ruminants have a higher metabolic rate and so require a higher caloric intake per unit of bodyweight than do larger ones. Their urgent energy demands can only be satisfied by a ready supply of nutritious and easily digestible browse that, on the shaded forest floor, tends to be scattered.

Very little is known about the red duiker, or indeed about any of the fourteen different species of duiker that inhabit Africa. The reason they remain a scientific mystery stems from the very inaccessibility which allows them to thrive. They are mainly nocturnal; they are also shy, dashing away in a surprisingly violent burst of energy at the least disturbance. With their stoopbacked posture, duikers, (an Afrikaans name meaning 'diver') are able to plunge into the thickest vegetation at astonishing speed. Living dispersed as they do

A grey duiker chews with great relish on a fallen marula berry found along a forest trail festooned with spider's webs, whose occupants wait poised with unmoving patience to seize insects that ensnare themselves.

means they occupy small territories they know intimately well, a great advantage when trying to elude predators.

These enigmatic little antelopes have a very ancient history, for primitive ruminants like them were among the first leaf-eating specialists to emerge in these forests 50 million years ago. It is this quality of antiquity that gives the forest and all its denizens a special appeal.

The wild lonely cry of a fisheagle echoed amongst the trees and I thought at the time how strange it was to hear its familiar voice in this waterless woodland, seeming so far from its usual haunts. In fact throughout the walk we had never been more than a few kilometres from the lake and at this point we were even closer than that. But other than the fisheagle's beguiling song there was no hint of the lake's proximity. Certainly no cooling breezes penetrated to ease the breathless heat and humidity. Under this assault Margot was left gasping but endured the sauna conditions without complaint and it was she who spotted the first epiphytic orchids.

Their flat, pale green stems entwined like ribbons through the branches of trees that acted as mechanical supports. Without looking hard we found two of the eight species that have been identified in False Bay Park. Both have white blossoms; one is small and thickly clustered, the other has larger flowers with salmon pink centres and forms a graceful arch against the lichen-decorated trunk of the host tree. Appearances apart, epiphytes are not parasitic but only use other plants as props without drawing energy from them. They take water directly from the moisture in the air through thin-walled aerial roots. Numerous species of ferns, lichens and orchids occupy this niche and so avoid competing with other plants on the shaded, root-filled floor.

Quietly rounding a corner we suddenly came face to face, for one frozen moment, with a pair of suni, male and female. The slender, lamb-sized antelope strained towards us, vibrant with tension, like coiled springs about to break loose. I had time to note that the male had thick, deeply ridged, backward sloping horns; the female was hornless; visible, too, were the prominent scent glands below their eyes, their pelage reddish-fawn. There was no question of reaching for my camera, the slightest movement – gone – not running together but in opposite directions, instantly out of sight. The meeting was breathtakingly brief but that was only to be expected and I took immense pleasure in sighting the creature described in a Natal Parks' leaflet as 'difficult to find as a rare jewel'.

Further along the trail I saw a red squirrel sprawled on a branch. As soon as it registered our presence it jerked to taut attention, legs braced, whisking its tail up and down in time to a defiant alarm chatter, then scurried away. This particular species of squirrel has a very limited distribution in South Africa and I had never seen one in the wilds before. So within half-an-hour I had added two new species to my personal mammal checklist. Together with the sighting at the beginning of the trail of a green coucal, an ornothological first, our day turned out to be highly successful.

Almost back at camp Margot caught my attention with a quiet hiss and when I turned she pointed stiffly to a bundle of red fur I had walked right past. It was a newborn bushbuck fawn 'lying out' – that is, left by its mother in hiding while she moved about her range attending to her affairs. The fawn relies on immobility to avoid detection but unlike its natural predators, we have colour vision and can distinguish between an object and its background.

At the click of the camera the fawn raised its head and opened huge black eyes to stare in astonishment at what must certainly have been the first humans it had ever seen. Then slowly, very cautiously, it rose to its feet, turned, and stole away in that characteristic hunchbacked bushbuck fashion, tiptoeing in that highstepping exaggerated parody of stealth I last saw in a movie cartoon.

It is occasions like this that make walking a wilderness so worthwhile. The opportunity exists for an intimacy never dreamed of in the normal course of events. I am not alone in wanting to bridge the chasm between technological man and wild beast. The situation is riddled with contradictions and ambiguities, but how wondrous to stretch out a hand, as naturalist Iain Douglas-Hamilton did, and touch the extended trunk of Virgo, a wild female elephant, in a physical act of faith that transcends aeons of interspecific enmity. That inspirational moment unfortunately has little to do with reality. During one of Douglas-Hamilton's absences from Lake Manyara, his Tanzanian elephant study area, Virgo was destroyed by poachers and he has, on more than one occasion, nearly been killed by wild animals that had no reason to trust his motives.

We were determined to make the most of the refreshing sea breeze and elected

Samango monkeys are confined to forests; they are more arboreal than their cousins, the vervets, and rarely forage on the ground; consequently they are difficult to photograph.

to sleep outside the tent that night. We sprayed ourselves sticky with insect repellant but the whine of mosquitoes homing in on their target filled our ears nonetheless. Towards midnight, with the fire's embers dimly glowing, the campsite was visited by a scavenging porcupine. I was alerted to its approach by the scraping of quills against metal as it passed under the car. It methodically shuffled nearer, constantly stopping to investigate and test the edibility of various items. I could clearly make out the silhouette of its heavy blunt head while its crest of quills luminously reflected the moonlight.

It drew nearer, either unaware or uncaring of me lying motionless so close by until, when it was only a metre or so from my face, I slowly sat up. The porcupine's response was immediate – turning full about it flared its formidable quills with a hollow rattle. When I made no further move it rushed off a few paces then repeated its display lest I had it in mind to take him while his defences

were down. Looking back to insure I intended no harm, he neatly settled his hackles and hurried into the night.

Lake St Lucia is also an extremely important waterbird breeding ground and we spent a day in a permanent hide that overlooked the bustling Hluhluwe River colony. This breeding site has probably been in existence for a long time and is the only one at St Lucia where wood storks have nested and, since 1962, the only site used by the great white egret, yellowbilled egret, grey heron and blackheaded heron. It is also the only place in South Africa where pinkbacked pelicans regularly breed.

Pinkbacked pelicans nest in trees, unlike their larger relative, the white pelican, which prefers a groundlevel scrape on St Lucia's islands. Since World War II when Catalina flying boats were based at the lake, human disturbance has had a serious adverse affect on bird breeding. In those days it was normal practice for Catalinas returning from a mission to clear their machineguns by firing on flocks of pelicans and basking crocodiles. Fishermen used pelican embryos as bait. In 1951 thousands of pelican eggs were found abandoned on Bird and Lane islands. In recent years military activities in the area might have caused the otherwise unexplained desertion of eggs by white pelicans in 1974 and 1978 and account for the decrease in the number of breeding Caspian terns.

The only way to get close enough to photograph the nervous greater flamingos wading the lake shallows was to set up my own hide. I pitched a tent among the phragmites at the water's edge and it worked perfectly. The unsuspecting birds fed to within 15 metres of me, their queer heads upside down, straining plankton from the saline soup with their bills' remarkable filtering mechanism. They muttered querulously amongst themselves while they worked and at sunset when I came out of hiding they rose up in alarm, splintering into feathered fragments with goose-like honks.

Flamingos are abundant in winter in the northern part of the lake around False Bay Park when salinity and the lake level is best suited to plankton. The highly specialized birds are only able to harvest plankton in the top five centimetres of water, leaving a huge surplus that attracts prawns which in turn attract fish that crocodiles prey on, creating a marvellously inter-dependent food chain.

From False Bay in the north we drove to Mapelane Nature Reserve at St Lucia's southern extremity. It is on the south bank of the Umfolozi River where it enters the sea and set in one of the best examples of coastal forest in Zululand. As soon as camp was made I set off to explore, holding as close to the river bank as the thick vegetation would permit.

The Umfolozi did not always flow directly into the sea. In 1952 it was diverted from St Lucia estuary in an effort to dispose of an accumulated silt load brought about by bad farming practices in the catchment area. The rechannelling of Umfolozi has been only partially successful in combating major siltation in St Lucia to which the other rivers, with the exception of Mkuzi, all contribute. Each year it becomes fractionally shallower. It has been estimated that at the present rate of deposition the lake could be filled to mean sea-level in little over a century.

Further upstream I used well worn hippo paths that made travelling much easier. Deep, waterfilled, three-toed hippo footprints were everywhere. On the river edge well consolidated mud had given rise to mangrove swamps. Red, stalk-eyed crabs hovered at the entrance to holes that riddled the firm mudbanks. Mudskippers, brown as the mud they inhabit with darker dappling, came out of the water to feed on insects and other in-

vertebrates that swarmed on the soft ooze. As I moved by they skittered back to the safety of the river.

Mudskippers breathe on land by holding water in their mouths from which they extract oxygen by swilling it with a rolling action of the head across their mouthlinings. They are also able to absorb some oxygen directly from the air through their moist skins. But these adaptations only permit them to remain out of water for a short time. After a few minutes they must return for another mouthful and a thorough soaking.

Crowned hornbills conversed in melancholy whistles. A family party of terrestrial bulbuls chattered quietly as they

searched for food among the fallen leaves on the forest floor. Nobody knows how old this forest is. Trees cling to dunes that roll back from the sea in sandy ridges so steep they have kept the forest in a near pristine state. Several years ago prospectors looking for titanium, zircon and rutile found rich ore deposits all along the coast and an extensive orebody lies buried beneath Mapelane. The only way heavy metals can be recovered here

This newly born bushbuck fawn opened huge black eyes to stare in astonishment at the first human it had ever seen. It rose to its feet in fright and tiptoed away in search of its mother.

St Lucia boasts an astonishing variety of
birds – 367 recorded species. An important
waterbird breeding ground, it is the only
place in South Africa where pinkbacked
pelicans regularly breed. Pinkbackeds, left,
nest in trees, unlike the white pelicans
which prefer a groundlevel scrape.

A goliath heron warily edges away from a
young crocodile seeking a place in the sun
while greater flamingos strain plankton
from the saline soup through the remarkable
filtering mechanism of their bills.
At sunset the flamingos rise up in
alarm with goose-like honks.

is by bulldozing away the superficial mantle of vegetation and topsoil to obtain the sand for further processing.

A decision whether or not to mine has yet to be finalized. One can only hope that this irreplaceable forest will be left in peace. What is needed is a balance between resources and progress, and a reaffirmation of our kinship with the Earth. Back at camp, settled around a log fire, the night was almost still. An occasional errant breeze guttered a flame that otherwise stood straight up and the smell of acacia woodsmoke permeated the air – an African aroma.

We prepared a favourite dinner – fresh farmyard chicken stuffed with onions and garlic cloves, sprinkled with rosemary, sage, crushed bay leaves and black pepper, then wrapped in tinfoil and roasted slowly over fat, hot coals.

No one spoke; words were superfluous. A bushbaby shrieked discordantly with the raucous abandonment of a distressed child.

Bushbabies, also known more specifi-cally as thick-tailed galagos, swarm in these forests. In our torch beam we picked out a group moving with grave deliberation amongst the branches of the trees that overhung our campsite. They stared down at us, curious and unafraid, their huge eyes absorbing the light.

What is remarkable about the bush-baby's eyes is not only their size but that they are in front of its face: a feature of primates. Like monkeys, apes and man they have five fingers and toes, each with a nail. Yet they are such primitive primates as to be really prosimians. Their cuddly, winsome appearance has changed very little since their beginnings more than 25 million years ago.

After lights out a rusty spotted genet visited to pick over the remains of the chicken carcass and next morning its tracks were clearly visible on the rain-softened ground. The shower had brought out various species of snails and millipedes – black and red ones – as well as brown woodlice busily excavating dead wood.

It was the rainy season and so we had Mapelane to ourselves. It was hard to leave but I had made arrangements with the ranger in charge of St Lucia's Eastern Shores Nature Reserve to accompany him on his monthly tour of inspection to the wild and prohibited Lake Bangazi district south of Sodwana Bay.

The broad paved highway from the hamlet of Mtubatuba to St Lucia township had been hacked through Duku-duku, the largest stand of coastal forest remaining in the territory. Dukuduku is a succinct Zulu name meaning 'the place of groping in the dark, trying to find a way out'.

In the old days, during times of insta-bility, local Zulu clans were in the habit of withdrawing themselves and their cattle to the forest's depths to wait out the troubles. Since then much of it has been replaced by pine plantations that now give way to fields of sugar cane which press hard against St Lucia village. A sign alongside the bridge spanning this narrow southern tip of the Lake cau-

Zululand's nights rustle with activity as nocturnal creatures go about their business. In common with all night animals, this prowling caracal's eyes have a tapetum membrane that reflects ambient light. The striped polecat is strictly nocturnal and therefore seldom seen. Its conspicuous colouring advises potential enemies to leave it alone – should the warning go unheeded the attacker is sprayed with a powerful jet of evil-smelling fluid from the polecat's anal gland. The hedgehog, middle, is omnivorous, bustling about in search of insects, small mice, eggs and wild fruit. When alarmed it curls into a tight ball, with spines erected to point outwards. The arboreal bushbaby's habitat is restricted to forests and thickets, its presence advertised by raucous screams.

tioned 'Beware of hippos crossing the road at night'.

We went over to the thin strip of land between Lake St Lucia and the Indian Ocean known, rather prosaically, as the Eastern Shores. In the past elephants migrated down this land bridge to ford a shallow portion of the lake at a point called Elephant Crossing by the Zulus, but referred to as Brodies Crossing by modern cartographers. The last recorded elephant shot there was as late as 1924. A herd came down again in 1937 but having failed in an attempt to cross it returned north to Tongaland. After that elephant were seen no more.

Towards the end of the year Eastern Shores' reed- and sedge-dominated swamps were the centre of focus for myriad nesting birds, performing the rites of spring. Red Bishop cocks self-consciously puffed out gorgeous red and black breeding plumage. They inspected the reedbeds in slow airy flight that, combined with the buzzing sound they made, suggested a gathering of fantastic bumblebees.

Eight different species of weavers built wonderfully intricate nests there, each species to its own design. An awkward young lesser masked weaver exhibited the comic ineptitude of a beginner – he knew what to do, but his co-ordination was hopeless. Where they consorted in colonies the clamour of so many excited birds was deafening.

Whenever we ate, the bright yellow, black visaged male masked weavers and drab hens would hop on to the table, cock

their heads from side to side to assess our reaction, then peck up our leavings.

On the initial trip to Eastern Shores I arrived in the last days of May when wild gladioli bloom red and orange. There were still a few days to go before heading north to Bangazi and I used the time to take a closer look at this southern tip.

I stayed atop Mount Tabor in the old concrete bunkhouse that started life in World War II as a Royal Air Force radar observation post to serve the anti-submarine Catalina aircraft stationed on Lake St Lucia. In 1943 a Catalina crashed shortly after take-off killing eight of the nine crew members. The wreck can still be seen near the eastern shore of the lake and, strangely, in 1959 pinkbacked pelicans nested on it instead of in the trees at their usual Hluhluwe River site.

I had a spectacular uninterrupted view of everything between the ocean and the lake. The land not under pine plantations comprises open, rolling grassland interspersed with remnant clumps of dune forest. Since 300 AD African pastoralists have cleared the indigenous forests to make fields for agriculture and obtain charcoal for their iron smelting; man-induced fires have also diminished the forest's extent. The pioneering African mangosteen, *Garcinia livingstonei*, saplings I discovered in the grasslands are a first indication that this was once all forest and will revert once again, if fire is kept out.

That night, in spite of a buffeting gale the sharp alarm whistles of agitated reedbuck ascended from the valley below; pockets of trapped wind caused shifts and stirrings; doors rattled and opened mysteriously; there was an eeriness about the place. It was not hard to imagine the ghosts of the dead airmen had taken possession of the blockhouse; it was after all the last building on their old base. Who knows? A friend whose opinion I greatly respect holds an abiding belief in a spiritual world that teems with poltergeists, swarming, sensed but unseen, all about us. He contends that if for a moment we acquired the extra sense needed to perceive them, the revelation could well drive us mad. A spotted eagle owl hooted diabolically in a way I'm sure I've never heard before. I went reluctantly to bed, wondering what had come over me.

The next morning, having survived the dangers of the night, I took the Mziki trail down to the lake shore. Reedbuck bounded away with their distinctive rocking-horse gait, tails lofting to reveal white undercoverts that flash in the sun, their shrill whistles tapering off in a series of gasps expelled by the force of landing after a leap. Sometimes as they run, they produce another extraordinary sound, like a cork drawn from a wine bottle, that comes from a pair of inguinal pouches between their hind legs.

With a population of about 5 000, Eastern Shores has the highest concentration of common reedbuck in Africa. In the absence of predators (cheetahs having only recently been re-introduced) startling colour variations have come about. I saw an all white ram standing stark against a green hillside. It was not an albino but the result of a shift in the ratio of hair shades that range in colour from black, brown, red to white, with less dark and more white hairs occurring than normal. Because pale reedbuck stand out instead of blending with their natural surroundings, predators usually select them. These white mutants are still very uncommon and I was lucky to see one, although in a natural context they must be regarded as defective.

I breakfasted on the deep purple, refreshingly astringent berries of the numerous umdoni trees and the succulent plums of the *landophia* creeper. A troop of arboreal samango monkeys watched me in discreet silence from the forest

In early summer St Lucia's reed and sedge dominated swamps are the centre of focus for myriad nesting birds. Top. An awkward young lesser masked weaver exhibits the ineptitude of a beginner – he knows what to do but his co-ordination is hopeless; and a red bishop cock flaunts its vibrant breeding plumage. This all-white reedbuck ram is not an albino but the result of a shift in the ratio of hair shades that range from black, brown, red to white, with more white hairs occurring than normal.

canopy. At the lake's edge I disturbed a big crocodile that waddled on short bowed legs into the water.

St Lucia Lake and its adjoining swamps are an ideal habitat for crocodiles to prey on migrating shoals of fish. For some 150 million years they have been the dominant predators of tropical lakes and rivers. They have come down from the Mesozoic age of the reptiles almost unchanged and resemble dinosaurs in all structural respects.

Crocodiles play an important role in maintaining St Lucia's aquatic ecology. They feed mainly on fish and help keep the population healthy by removing the sick and the weak. They concentrate on the slow-moving barbel which in turn eat tilapia fry. The extermination of crocodiles from certain rivers has disrupted finely balanced ecosystems and has had an adverse effect on fish production.

Recent research has shown that crocodile social life is more complex than was suspected. In particular the relationship between a mother and her young has ex-

cited the imagination of people previously inclined to dismiss the magnificent monster as vermin. On a subsequent trip I was fortunate enough to witness the remarkable maternal instincts possessed by so unlikely a candidate.

A grey monstrous old female had selected a nesting site well above the waterline. One night she laid about 50 eggs into a shallow pit she had scraped in the sand. The protective mother remained in close proximity to the nest throughout the three-month incubation period. She spent the time virtually without food, seeming to fall into a sort of trance. It is during brief absences when she must hunt that the eggs become vulnerable to predation from monitor lizards and mongoose.

When the eggs were close to hatching the young within began to make loud piping calls that could be heard, through shell and sand, from several metres away. The female was stimulated by the chorus to uncover the eggs and as the hatchlings struggled to the surface she

tenderly picked them up in her jaws with a quick gulping motion. With a second lift of her head she manoeuvred them into the gular pouch that suspends from the bottom of her mouth. As the weight of her cargo increased the pouch hung like a large bag between her jaws.

She cracked open unhatched eggs in her mouth to liberate the youngsters inside and it was awesome to see those tiny leftover dinosaurs peering out with reptilian composure from behind a palisade of teeth, ready to go into the world. She ferried them to a nursery area amongst floating vegetation where they would remain for several months, with the mother continuing to guard them during their first few weeks in the water.

Few wild animals have been so revered and reviled. The ancient Egyptians deified and sought to propitiate them. Some of the temples at Abu Simbel were dedicated to this biblical leviathan and thousands of embalmed crocodile mummies were placed in sacred repositories. But for the most part crocodiles are held

to be loathesome and dangerous. Their public image has not been improved by their readiness to dine on human flesh if the opportunity arises.

Frederick Findlay, an early European visitor to St Lucia, wrote, surprisingly: 'it is a peculiar fact that the natives (of this district), have no fear of the lake crocodiles. They often wade waist-deep across at a spot where the water is shallow . . . to visit a kraal on the other side, and the women go far out into the water to gather certain waterplants, but it is said they are never molested. This is all the more striking when we bear in mind that a Zulu is very chary about entering any of the inland lagoons, pools, or rivers, having a wholesome dread of the crocodiles that lurk in their dark waters.'

There is a grave behind the old mission station at Mission Rocks on the Eastern Shores that tells a different story. In March 1902, shortly after Findlay's visit, a Norwegian missionary, Olsen Lindfeldt, set out from Mission Rocks on his way back to Europe. For

Like a tiny left-over dinosaur, a hatchling crocodile, left, peers out from between its mother's palisade of teeth with reptilian composure, ready to go into the world.

Above. The female's gular pouch sags with the weight of her cargo of hatchlings and cracked egg shells. Young crocodiles, having been carefully 'mothered' in their nest during a three-month incubation, liberate themselves from the egg by chipping away with the eggtooth on the end of their jaws, specially designed for the purpose. If they experience difficulties in escaping their piping calls alert the female who picks them up, and using her teeth as gently as forceps, applies sufficient pressure to crack the shells.

three years he had laboured in Africa and now he was going home to marry his fiancée; he decided to wade the lake on the underwater ridge at Brodie's Crossing. Although the local Zulus had warned him not to attempt it alone he chose to ignore them. He hadn't gone far when a big crocodile exploded out of the water and siezed him by the thigh. His screams for help alerted the Zulus within earshot to his plight. They scared off the crocodile and carried the grievously wounded man back to the mission station where he died the following day at the age of 32. He thus became the first recorded white man killed by a crocodile in Zululand.

Some victims of crocodile attacks live to tell their harrowing tale. A young Zulu girl drawing water from the Mfazana (Little Wife) pan on the Eastern Shores had her wrist grabbed by a small crocodile. She struggled in vain to free herself until in desperation she bit it on the nose whereupon it released its grip.

In the late 1960s at Sengwana Point in St Lucia a Zulu child was taken and eaten. Her undigested remains were recovered from the crocodile's stomach after it was shot by the warden – grisly evidence of its culpability. It is around incidents like these that the tribal myths and legends concerning St Lucia's prehistoric amphibians have grown.

Mission Rocks has become a Natal Parks outpost and the regional ranger – now warden – was Tony Tomkinson, a man typical of game rangers in many ways – stocky, tough, dedicated and a better than average shot. Untypically he is also colourfully articulate, with an alert, lucid imagination. Nor is he a man short of ideas. In the little time I spent in his company I came to know him as one of the best of a good breed.

Tony had some hippo culling to attend to and invited me along. St Lucia has the largest southern concentration of hippo in Africa, some 600 animals. During the day they prefer to congregate in the lake where there is a supply of fresh water and to come ashore at night to graze the Eastern Shores' prolific grasslands. But there is a limit to how many hippos St Lucia can support. Fences that keep animals out of neighbouring farmlands also prevent migration from overgrazed areas. Animal populations

which grow too large for a reserve must be regulated. Where man-made restrictions interfere it is a fallacy to believe that natural areas will right themselves. It is now recognized that given the right circumstances our depleted mammal populations have a remarkable ability to 'bounce back', unlike vegetation and soils which take many years to form.

Regular visitors to game parks, inevitably enthusiastic preservationists, content to admire the herds of hippo and antelope, are now being asked to become environmentalists, to appreciate the impact the herds are having on their habitat and to accept the need for remedial culling where necessary. But the old 'let Nature-take-care-of-her-own' approach has been tried and within the restricted confines of today's parks simply does not work.

'Culling isn't sporting,' Tony said as

we drove past the Cape Vidal tourist camp, heading north, 'it isn't supposed to be. The idea is to get the job done as efficiently and painlessly as possible.' And so it was.

We met up with Brian Harris, who came across from Charter's Creek on the western side of the lake to lend a hand. Only one hippo was to be taken out on that operation: Brian made the shot and that was all it took, just one shot. He selected a target a little apart from the main herd to minimize disturbance and within minutes the slain animal bobbed to the surface, pink belly uppermost, legs in the air.

Tony and the head game guard stripped to their briefs and paddled out in a canoe to get a rope on the carcass to tow it ashore. They worked close to the herd which followed their progress with bel-

lows and gaping yawns. There was a flurry of excitement when it looked like the dominant bull was about to charge; Tony snatched up his rifle and covered him, but the bull thought better of it.

I have been out on a number of culling operations but am still unable to approach the task in hand with emotional detachment. There is that terrible existential moment between a thing living and the crack of the shot that extinguishes the cleverness of its brain. During the countdown a corruption of a line from Dylan Thomas – 'Go gently into that good night' – reverberated in my mind like a pantheist incantation and was only stilled by the roar of the rifle.

Culling is absolutely necessary but it is also an unpleasant business. Some hold that, like Victorian sex, it's all right as long as you don't enjoy it. Be that as it may, after as many as possible surplus animals have been removed by live capture, there is no alternative to shooting.

There is a new awareness amongst wildlife managers that if game parks are to survive into the land-hungry future they will not only have to provide direct benefits to tribes people living on their borders, but might also have to become economically viable, which they certainly are not right now. One proposal, to permit supervised recreational hunting in parks, could be their single greatest source of revenue. It is also highly controversial. Traditionalists liken it to holding a rock concert in a cathedral and deplore what they see as a mercenary dollars-and-cents approach to nature conservation. It would be ironic if misguided but well-intentioned sentimentalists thwarted the implementation of the

Culling is an unpleasant business. Where burgeoning animal populations threaten their own habitat, control measures are absolutely necessary. St Lucia supports approximately 600 hippos, the largest southern concentration in Africa, but to prevent overgrazing their numbers must be regulated. St Lucia's warden, Tony Tomkinson, wades towards the bobbing carcass to attach a rope before towing it ashore.

revolutionary policies needed for wildlife to survive in Africa's deteriorating social and economic climate.

My attitude towards recreational hunting, or culling for that matter, may seem anomalous but it is not. In principle I am not against either, in fact, for strictly pragmatic reasons, I am all in favour. The arguments in their support are irrefutable. I don't hunt myself because of a suggestion put to me by my grandfather when I was still young.

My grandfather died years ago, but I remember him as a Disneyesque idealisation of the archetypal wise old man. He had a full and successful life. When I was a child he could thrill me with tales of hunting adventures during World War I while stalking von Lettow-Vorbeck's elusive army against the vast splendid backdrop of what was then German Tanganyika.

He smoked a pipe as he talked, staring all the while into the middle distance, as if dredging up those kind memories from the deepest recesses of his mind. He had a habit of punctuating his stories with thoughtful pauses, which lent an air of precision, of concern for accuracy to the telling and heightened the drama.

It was because of his hunting yarns that I felt confident of an ally in a quarrel I was having with my parents. They objected to my turning my pellet gun on the flocks of doves inhabiting the scrub behind our house. I felt sure of his approval for by restricting myself to doves, a quarry difficult to stalk in the first place, once the shooting was done the felled bird could be ceremoniously plucked, grilled over an open fire and eaten. For those reasons my hunting forays seemed to me to be not only justifiable but righteously commendable.

When I presented my case, my grandfather brought out his pipe, fired it up, then sat sucking contemplatively. Finally he said, 'Next time you go out shooting I want you to try something. Once you've got the dove lined up in your sights and you know that all you have to do is squeeze the trigger and it'll

Zebras have been re-introduced to
St Lucia's False Bay Park where they
again go about their affairs as they have
in this area through the millennia.

drop dead – don't fire. Lay your gun down and watch what it does now that you've given it a chance to go on living.'

He said no more and although I promised to do as he asked I was uneasy. I suspected what the outcome would be and foresaw an end to my hunting career almost before it had started.

And so it was. Having set my gun aside I watched as the dove ruffled its wings and began preening, the black ring of feathers circling its neck straining against a full crop. Then it called that harsh 'coo' so characteristic of the African bush. I understood the message for what it was – a celebration of life. To this day, whenever I hear that poignant pure song, there comes a deep wave of memory, almost an echo, of that moment of revelation. As I had anticipated I never hunted again and have never had cause to regret it.

That night there came the distant sound of rolling thunder and I worried that our Bangazi trip might get washed out. But the storm never materialized and we departed next morning in a burst of bright sunshine.

North of Cape Vidal Tony and I drove along the coastline, 79 kilometres of which was proclaimed in 1979 as the St Lucia Marine Reserve. The sanctuary extends from the low water mark for three kilometres out to sea. When it was established there was very little life left on the reefs; crayfish and octopus had disappeared, small marine fish were virtually non-existent and mussels had been almost completely stripped off the rocks.

After only a year's protection the situation improved dramatically; sea lice and crabs increased to staggering proportions; young mussels and crayfish came back, along with marine and reef fish. Portuguese sardines, not seen for many years, came down in huge shoals, followed by gamefish.

At one point Tony stopped to peer through his binoculars at an outboard anchored off-shore, then, satisfied there was no poaching, gave a wave and we went on our way. Caspian terns, with large red bills and jet crowns, floated on the sea breeze. They occur all along the southern African coastline but are everywhere sparsely distributed except at St Lucia where they are abundant.

At Sodwana Bay National Park we

turned inland again. I had several months earlier spent just one night at Sodwana – it is too popular with fishermen for my taste. I had wanted to explore the silent dune forests, but the noisy crowds let me know I had judged the timing badly.

Beyond the forest we followed a sandy track that winds over undulating grass-capped dunes laid down by shoreline and wind processes following a receding Pleistocene sea. There was no one there except us. The area is used as a missile testing range and the tribes people who had lived there have been relocated. It is administered jointly by the military, the Forestry Department and Natal Parks, each attending to those concerns under their jurisdiction. Together with St Lucia, which it adjoins, the Bangazi district forms the largest contiguous wilderness area in Zululand – greater than the Umfolozi-Hluhluwe complex. But it is threatened by titanium strip-mining and pine afforestation. Because it is not open to tourism, unfortunately not enough people know about it to make its welfare a public issue.

The Landcruiser flushed a rare pink-throated longclaw that settled again a short distance away. A pair of side-striped jackals got up and raced along-side us for a moment, then broke away. The fruit-eating sidestriped jackal is more nocturnal and larger than its black-backed cousin. There, in reverse of the normal situation, it is the more common of the two, thriving in this coastal mosaic of grassland, savanna and thickets.

The sight of a wary Stanley bustard stalking along in search of insects, prompted Tony to tell how he earned his Zulu nickname. 'When I first joined the department my Zulu was very poor and trying to make myself understood I mispronounced a word I had looked up earlier in a phrasebook, so that instead of asking 'Do you speak English?' it came out, 'Do you speak the language of the ground hornbill?' Ever since that time the game guards have called me 'the ground hornbill that thunders' although I don't know what the second half of the name refers to.'

I suspect it almost certainly alludes to his prowess as a marksman and hunter. Zulu nicknames usually relate to a physical characteristic such as 'long beard' or, for spectacle wearers 'four-eyes' but one very trepid biologist visiting Umfolozi was ignomoniously labelled 'the cockroach's antenna'.

As we approached the sedge-lined Bangazi North Lake where Tony had built a one-roomed wooden hut and where we slept that night, a marsh harrier started up, a wriggling frog grasped firmly in its talons. In the fringing swamp forest a flight of rameron pigeons boomed overhead and a shy grey duiker doe watched from the edge of the tree-line – the only wildlife that survived the intensive poaching pressures of the past are the small, the nocturnal and the secretive. Tony was pleased to see that populations are again rallying. The last hippo in the lake was shot in 1973 but since then it has been recolonized by five hippo that migrated the 15 kilometres from the Mkuzi swamps.

In the glow of a pink and orange sunset we settled round a fire with frosty cans of beer and roasted the raw peanuts I had bought from Tonga peasants in Sodwana. An unseen redwing francolin racketed hysterically, stopping abruptly at the top of its call, as if it had forgotten its complaint. Tony was saying how important it was that Bangazi, one of Zululand's last unspoilt wild places, be preserved in its natural state and somehow that call seemed even more appropriate.

Tony Tomkinson has a profound sense of the real meaning of wilderness. In his 15 years service with Natal Parks he has worked in the best parts of Zululand and seen all the changes that have come to pass. Considering recent developments have come so fast he could be termed a young 'old Africa hand'. He was there when it was still pristine; wild animals and unsophisticated people, inside and outside the game parks. He was wise enough to recognize that what others took for granted was rapidly disappearing. He taught himself to sit still, to absorb the sights and sounds, the doomed majesty of it all – squirrelling away vignettes of old Africa, drawing it into himself, out of love and respect.

At Ndumu, one of his earliest posts, he regularly canoed across the Usutu River to Moçambique to look up the Portuguese

District Commissioner there. They would confer on poaching and witchcraft cases, swop anecdotes and sink a goodly number of Laurentina beers together.

'Bloody DC,' he affectionately recalled. 'He's the reason I never spent my first night in Moçambique sober. We didn't speak much of each others' language, but we got along well enough.'

At that point Tony, who until now had been gazing into the fire's glowing coals suddenly sat bolt upright.

'Wonder what became of him after Frelimo?' A rhetorical question, asked in astonishment, as if the thought had just struck him. 'I've never been back, but I heard they've all gone, except the Indian who ran the trading store. His people originally came from Goa but I guess after all this time he feels he belongs in Africa, as we all do.'

I stared into the night; above there was a forest of stars; below, somewhere, a rare brown hyena prowled – we had ear-

lier found its scats. 'I wonder if it could happen here?' Tony reflected, so quietly I assumed he was talking to himself.

We set out next morning in a turquoise-dawn in the hope of finding elusive bushpigs before they retired for the day and instead surprised a nocturnal white-tailed mongoose still out on its rounds. Larks, quail, warblers and cisticolas were already awake and announcing a new day. The sun rose, hot as Latin blood, into a faultless blue sky.

Tony gestured around us. 'How's that for MMBA?' he asked, quoting the expression I had used in the Etosha book – 'miles and miles of bloody Africa' said with gruff affection.

In an increasingly crowded world it is easy to forget that places like this still exist. Nothing interrupts the landscape; from horizon to horizon there are no points of reference; just a sea of billowing grass studded with archipelagos of forest and us, tiny molecules, adrift.

A white pelican attends to its ablutions.

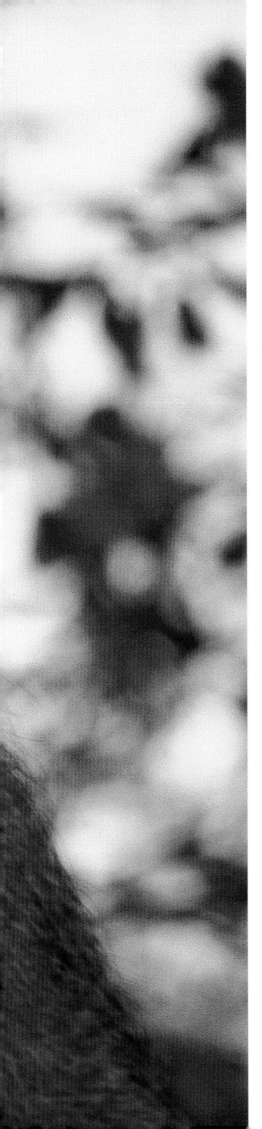

THE TRIBE THAT GREW TAILS

'He (the dog baboon) is a born bully,
a born criminal, a born candidate for the
hangmen's noose . . . He is as submissive as
a bulldozer, as gentle as a power-driven
lawnmower. He has the yellow-to-amber
eyes that one associates with
a riverboat gambler.'

Robert Ardrey – The Territorial Imperative

There is an aloe-studded, redstone krantz overlooking a thickly wooded dry water course near the Mtshopi entrance gate to Mkuzi Game Reserve. A troop of about 25 chacma baboons regularly retire to the safety of the cliff face to roost at night although I did not know that when I first pitched my tent on the cleared ground below. Before sun-up the next morning I drove out to get the feel of this new country. To the late-rising baboons the sight of my unguarded supplies was too tempting to ignore. By the time I returned the baboons had come and gone, their looting complete. They had invaded the tightly zippered tent by wriggling under the flaps and then proceeded to thoroughly ransack the place. Cardboard cartons of fruit juice were ripped open, apparently paddled in, and dark, sticky footprints were left all over the bedding. The raiders then embarked on a feeding frenzy. Any food not locked away was eaten except unripe fruit and vegetables, which were discarded after a testing bite. Biscuits were gobbled down, and crumbs were scattered everywhere. Canned goods had been hurled about in a pique of frustration – what couldn't be consumed was despoiled. Nothing was sacred. Clothing and toiletries lay scattered around and one of the baboons, perhaps the troop intellectual, had seemingly paused to glance through my copy of Henry Thoreau's 'Walden'. Gazing about at the destruction through a red film of rage, I notched a point on the downside of my precarious love-hate relationship with man's closest relative in southern Africa.

It was my own fault of course, I should have been more careful and after that I was; despite the inconvenience all food was stowed in the car. I left the tent open so that the baboons could inspect the bare larder without having to break in and perhaps rip the canvas. After my departure each morning they would file down and pick through the garbage. Though my leavings were poor they refrained from venting their disappointment on my camping paraphernalia. Their conduct was altogether more restrained than their introductory visit. On that occasion, perhaps excited by the bounteous food cache and nervously aware of the consequences if caught at their criminal behaviour, they had run

Life during a troop's day is dominated by the search for food. Baboons have an extremely varied diet that ranges from grass, herbs and fruit to termites, grasshoppers and other insects. But if feeding seems an incessant affair so are grooming sessions – an activity that not only maintains scrupulous hygiene but also reinforces social bonds.

Young baboons sail through the air with the greatest of ease. Although they spend much of their lives at groundlevel they depend on trees for security. To this end they possess two very useful abilities – a talent for judging distances and a capacity for grabbing hold of branches. Their forward-facing eyes are both able to focus on the same object and their grasping fingers permit them as much freedom of movement above the ground as on it.

amuck, as baboons sometimes will. Later, they came to recognize that I would tolerate their comings and goings as long as they acted with decorum. So we settled into a cordial truce and I soon learnt to appreciate my sickle-tailed neighbours and their preposterous antics.

One morning, instead of setting out as I usually did I remained in camp to bring my notes up-to-date. Sitting in the warm winter sunshine behind a collapsible table, cup of coffee in hand and gathering my thoughts, I could clearly watch the baboons' progress as they descended the krantz and swarmed into the tall trees fringing the campsite. Their expressive, dog-like faces peered down at me from the screening dark green foliage of the high branches. At first they were content to wait patiently for my departure but when it became apparent I did not intend leaving, their restless fidgeting intensified until they had whipped themselves into near hysteria. Adults hurled insults, roared threats; spoiled youngsters shrieked despairingly. Branches were angrily shaken. Several adult males rushed along the branches baring their formidable canine teeth in half-hearted attack displays. Then as suddenly as it had started the uproar subsided. Several animals dropped to the ground, casting sheepish

sidelong glances in my direction, then proceeded to play and groom as if I didn't exist. One adventurous young fellow nonchalantly sidled closer but at a warning grunt from his mother he turned tail and fled screeching in terror although I hadn't made a move. His cries set the whole troop off on a new round of demonstrating. Anyone who spends time in baboon company becomes familiar with their volatile temperaments. They are passionate creatures to the very core of their being.

Once they had accepted that they were not to have the free run of my camp that day they began drifting away across the savanna, foraging as they went. From the flora about them they selected a variety of leaves, berries, wild fruits, roots, grasses, tubers, bulbs and even flowers. Being omnivorous, animal food such as insects, scorpions, centipedes, lizards, birds eggs and fledglings were also eagerly snapped up. If the opportunity arises the newborn lambs of bushbuck, nyala, impala and steenbuck together with hares may be killed and eaten though they are little inclined to look for meat. Field naturalists have noted that baboons will not feed off an untended leopard or lion kill they may chance upon.

I was still at my paperwork late that afternoon when the troop returned to the

krantz with enough time in hand before nightfall to indulge in a little socializing – a favourite recreation. Individuals formed into clusters, usually with one or two adults at the centre, then began an intensely pleasurable grooming session. The groomers technique is highly efficient. Using both its hands and teeth it combs through the fur, collecting insects, dead skin (both of which it eats) and dirt. The groomee relaxes with a look of sheer bliss on its face, occasionally lifting a limb or rolling over to permit the groomer to get at a new spot. At twilight they gradually began to ascend the cliff where they spent the night lightly sleeping in a hunched-over sitting position. Baboons come equipped with flat, hard, insensitive pads of skin on their rumps, called 'ischial callosities' which permit them to spend the night upright in relative comfort. After they had settled down the only sound other than an occasional fuzzy murmur was the persistent, hacking cough of a member that had evidently caught a distressingly severe winter cold.

Scientists tell us that the forebears of man are from much the same stock as baboons; however, African folklore holds the connection between the two to be closer than that. One of the most popular Zulu legends maintains that ba-

boons are really degenerate men and women, whose tribal name was the Tusi. They were notoriously lazy, preferring to sit and talk all day rather than till the fields like their more industrious neighbours. When their food ran out they took advantage of their fellow-Zulus' traditionally hospitable natures to beg from them.

The Tusis were ridiculed for their indolence and finally, their pride sufficiently injured, decided to work like other people to insure their independence. They set off enthusiastically, first

talking a blacksmith into supplying them with pickheads through which they inserted stout sticks as handles. Next they borrowed seed and for the first few days were hard at work. But as muscles, unaccustomed to manual labour, began to ache, so their good intentions withered. They broke off hoeing to discuss whether to continue or not, leaning with their backs against the pickhandles as they did so. They decided to give it one more try after their long rest. Turning to take up their picks they discovered to their horror that the picks

turned with them – the handles had become grafted to their backs while the heads were rooted firmly in the soil. They frantically twisted from left to right, jumped and pulled only to have the heads break off and remain in the ground while the handles stuck permanently to their bodies. Then, ultimate calamity! Hair started growing on the handles and soon spread all over them. They hardly seemed human any more.

So ludicrous did they now look that all who saw them laughed out loud. They were told it served them right and their neighbours refused to help any more. Overcome by humiliation, the Tusis abandoned their homes and sought refuge in the wilderness. They have remained there ever since, having learnt to live off the land. Yet all the while they keep a practised eye on other people's villages, waiting for the corn to ripen in the gardens. When it does they sneak in and help themselves, rather than ask for it as they did in the past.

As hunter-gatherers, the Khoisan lived closer to nature in its basic form than did the pastoralist Zulus. They maintained an almost mystic affinity with their environment and its denizens. They thought of baboons as 'people who sit on their heels' and claimed they had a complex language all of their own. They were, however, too shrewd to converse in front of a White man lest they be press-ganged into working for him.

Few wild creatures are as ubiquitous as are baboons. I have found them thriving in habitats as diverse as semi-arid bush to tropical forest, from sea-level to the slopes of high mountains. Depending on whether the drill and mandrill of the West African forests are included there are five or seven species of baboon, ranging from the Cape Peninsula right up into Ethiopia and Sudan and across the Red Sea into Saudi Arabia.

Baboons originated with other monkeys in the Oligocene age, 35 million years ago. They are thought to have originally been forest dwellers.

With the onset of a drier climatic cycle reducing the forests' area, baboons gravitated onto the burgeoning savannas rather than remain in the forests and compete for a diminishing resource. But to survive in open country necessitated a restructuring of their social organization. To pinpoint and confront dangerous predators, baboons banded together in troops of between 10 and 100 individuals. The social bonds that developed

Baby baboons are born with conspicuous black coats and contrasting pink faces and ears, which may partly account for their irresistible attractiveness to other troop members. This female approaches a youngster uttering characteristic sounds that signal friendliness and interest; though she may attempt to touch it she will probably settle for grooming the mother in order to remain close to the baby.

were one of their most important survival prerequisites for it was not numbers alone that made for success. The way the troop functioned, how its members related to each other and together met the challenges of their world was the key to their proliferation.

I was intrigued by and wanted to see for myself the extent to which cohesion within baboon society was established through internal organization and the inter-relationships among individuals. Having arrived at a working accommodation with the Mtshopi troop I made up my mind to devote some of my time accompanying them on their daily rounds. To this I could add observations made from a hide overlooking one of Mkuzi's permanent waterholes which acted as a magnet to an astonishing assortment of creatures during the dry season.

Visiting waterholes, which baboons do daily, is usually the single most dangerous event of their day and attended to as speedily as possible. However, Mkuzi's small size, only 25 091 hectares, is unable to support lions or even many leopards. Here baboons are free to spend their mid-day break relaxing, socializing or simply trying the patience of other animals coming down to drink.

In Umfolozi, although I was able to photograph some aspects of baboon behaviour, most of the troops were wary of humans, especially anyone on foot, as I usually was. This state of affairs probably had everything to do with the abrasive relations that existed between them and the tribes people living beyond the park's boundaries, whose vegetable gardens they persistently raided. Because of their destructiveness to crops baboons in

During the course of their day, troop members are alert to signs of danger, relying on their superior eyesight, several times the magnification of man's, to spot an approaching predator. A leopard wishing to dine on baboon must first avoid the intense surveillance net, then streak in, seize an unsuspecting youngster and be gone before an alarm bark rallies the adult males. If the leopard is not quick enough the males will mob it and, ignoring personal danger, tear it to pieces.

Although squabbles are constantly breaking out amongst troop members, the disputes are usually quickly settled. When attacked by an older and stronger opponent this sub-adult's bloodcurdling screech attracted the attention of a dominant male who kept an eye on the scuffle. When the youngster took a bite on his back, the adult male forcefully intervened by separating the protagonists and restoring order.

Young baboons overflow with vigour and mischief – if two adolescents arrive at the end of a branch at the same time they delight in trying to push each other off. Although the skirmish is energetically contested, there are no hard feelings; in the next encounter the tables might well be turned.

most parts of Africa outside game parks are classified as 'vermin' and shot indiscriminately.

Any animal so full of character and observable commonsense as the baboon is a delight to watch. They are also incorrigible pranksters, not only amongst themselves but in their dealings with their fellow creatures. Their brains have developed to become curious enough to be called intelligent. They are tough, aggressive and adaptable; admirable qualities if they are to survive the murderous hurly-burly of savanna life. Yet baboons are far from being completely ground-dwelling primates – they remain dependent on trees for their security. To this end they have retained two extremely useful abilities – a talent for judging distances and a capacity for grabbing hold of branches. They have a pair of forward-facing eyes that can both focus on the same object. Their stereoscopic vision, binocular and in colour, is a great advance over most other African creatures. Their hands have grasping fingers which permit them almost as much freedom of movement high above the ground as it does on it.

The Mtshopi troops' day begins well after sunrise, as does that of most baboons. This is probably to avoid the menace of lurking predators, many of which are most active in the early hours. Although large predators in Mkuzi are few, it seems old habits die hard.

The youngsters were first to descend from the cliff face and began playing on the ground below. The older juveniles, between one to three or four years, spent little time during the day with their mothers, preferring to move, eat and play with others their own age. In no particular order the remaining members leisurely made their way to the base of the krantz where they split into smaller groups. Much as humans meet to converse, so baboons gather into groups to maintain compatible relations in their own baboon fashion.

This was one of the best times for me to photograph social interactions. Some members groomed each other while others just sat quietly. One group consisted of a female with a newly-born 'black' infant, surrounded by interested onlookers. All animals in the troop were groomed at some point but babies were groomed particularly frequently.

Baby baboons are born after a six-month gestation period and seem to be irresistibly attractive to other troop members, particularly females. The baby's attractiveness may partly result from its appearance; the pink face and ears contrasting with the black coat is very conspicuous against its mother's fawn pelt. On seeing an infant, other members approach the mother uttering characteristic grunts that signify friendliness and interest; they may groom the mother and also attempt to groom the baby. In this way the infant gets acquainted with the members of the troop at an early age, learns the social position of each individual and so becomes integrated into the society.

Once social courtesies are observed

the troop becomes restless, with some members setting off away from the krantz. Early researchers suggest that a baboon troop moving across country has a distinct order of progression with individuals taking up positions according to rank and sex as a defence strategy against predators. Later studies dispute this but what is certain is the role adult males play when predators are confronted.

While following three male cheetahs one mid-morning through Umfolozi's Gqoyini Valley their path crossed that of a baboon troop. I was in a car and the baboons took no notice of me but their reaction to the cheetahs, barely visible in the tall yellow grass, was immediate – a sudden barrage of loud, plosive alarm barks. The adult males bellowed deep,

harsh challenges and while the rest of the troop scurried to safety, they set about assessing the potential danger by climbing into trees and looking around. If it had been a serious threat such as a leopard the males would have grouped together and advanced in an aggressive manner, exposing their wicked canines, screeching and grunting. But in this case, once they realized that only cheetahs were involved, the males marched in a phalanx towards them without bothering to resort to threat posturing. It was enough for the disconcerted cats who trotted away without a moment's hesitation, casting nervous glances back over their shoulders as they fled. Faced with the troop's highly effective early warning system, backed up by their pug-

nacious temperament, most predators prefer to pick off stragglers, such as inexperienced juveniles or sick animals.

The troop is the association established by nature for the supply of a baboon's everyday wants. It is the only life feasible. Without it, existence would be perilous in a way a member within its security rarely knows. A baboon's emotional wellbeing depends on constant companionship – from the moment it is born there is hardly a time when there is not another baboon close by.

Within the troop there are several complex relationships among individuals that ensure a viable and successful way of life. Although dominant males rule a group they are not despots but rather are responsible for the prevention of fighting and the general welfare of the group. Their rule is not based only on brute strength but more on the force of their 'personalities'. Two or more males form a coalition or 'central hierarchy' which, as a unit, dominates all other males and other troop members as well. Such relationships may last for a period of time but then a series of fights will often reverse the males' positions whereas the status of females is stable and enduring.

I have never spent long in baboon company without the tranquility of the bush being shattered by an outburst of shrieks and barks. Quarrels are constantly erupting between juveniles but if they become too serious adults rush to the scene to separate the opponents. In fact there is very little real fighting amongst baboons. There are disputes and constant outbreaks of clamour but they are mostly mere noise. But what noise! Youngsters screech when they are punished as though they were being murdered on the spot. Yet for all their terrified tantrums they don't remain disciplined for long.

Young baboons are overflowing with vigour and mischief and are infinitely entertaining to watch at play. Roughhousing is the most popular kind of game, with running, wrestling and chasing – all activities that develop reflexes and muscles – being favoured group sports. Youngsters also seem to find falling from a tree highly satisfying. One will resolutely climb a tree, walk to the end of a branch, dangle desperately by one hand, drop to the ground, pick himself up and immediately repeat the performance. If two adolescents arrive at the end of a branch at the same time they try their utmost to push and drag each other off. Although the skirmish is energetically contested, there are no hard feelings; in the next encounter the tables might be turned.

Baboons have an unusual relationship with bushbuck and nyala, for though they have been recorded killing and eating the young of both species, the adult antelopes do not avoid baboon company. In fact, particularly during certain times of the year, they seek it out and are frequently seen beneath trees in which baboons are feeding, eating dislodged fruit and leaves. When feeding together their combined alertness – the baboon's superb eyesight, several times the magnification of man's, plus the antelope's superior sense of smell and hearing – makes for a very effective surveillance system. Similarly at waterholes baboons, antelope, zebra and giraffe rely to an extent on the other species' particular talent for discovering a lurking predator and all feel more confident when there is an assortment of animals drinking.

It is at waterholes that a baboon's relations with other animals can best be observed. Baboons know intimately the habits and tempers of their fellow creatures; bullying some, giving way to others and sometimes merely teasing, testing the response or even playing with another species. Sitting quietly in the hide at Mkuzi's Msinga pan provided me with hours of delight and fascination.

Warthogs are particularly numerous in Mkuzi and dealings with baboons are less than cordial. They tolerate each other at a distance of 10 metres or so and their groups partially intermingle without altercation but at other times warthogs chase baboons, even adult males. When this happens, the baboons quickly get out of the way, but without barking or showing any other sign of alarm.

Sitting in the hide at Msinga one early afternoon I watched a troop of baboons lounging in the loose, washed sand, more enervated than anything else, with only an occasional desultory squabble erupting. An old dog baboon, like an introspective geriatric taking the sun on a park bench, sat apart from the rest of the troop, basking in a slanted shaft of fil-

tered winter sunshine that pierced the woodland canopy. This was as typical a scene as any during the course of a baboon's stimulating day.

Although survival on the savanna is a constant struggle for most creatures, baboons nevertheless manage to forage and groom, fornicate and play in what appears to be a marvellously full, satisfying and endlessly entertaining life.

Baboons often associate with other animals whose alertness supplements their own. Their relationship with bushbuck, however, goes one step further: these antelope frequently wait beneath a tree where baboons are feeding to snap up dislodged fruit and leaves. At waterholes baboons and warthogs sometimes intermingle without altercation but at other times warthogs will chase baboons, even adult males.

FROM MKUZI TO NDUMU

*'No hillside without its grave,
no valley without its shadow'*
Zulu Proverb

There is a rhythm to dying just as there is to living – only the process is reversed. Death creeps up stealthily; at first a hardly perceptible disintegration and desiccation that gradually accelerates until its terminal objective is plain to see. This is as true of inanimate matter as it is of the incarnate.

It was September in Mkuzi Game Reserve and all the land waited for rain. I spent my days attending the rainwater pan at Malibali, a vigil that had assumed the intimacy of a deathwatch. Each day evaporation and the thirsty wildlife drew off a little more of their lifeblood, the pan's diminishing water supply.

In the beginning the water's surface area seemed virtually inviolate. It served as home to a pair of Egyptian geese and a number of waders. Each morning hordes of terrapins hauled out of its brown

Eventually, all wildlife attends the rainwater pan at Malibali but each day evaporation and thirsty animals draw off a little more of its life-giving water. Alongside, freshwater turtles, or terrapins, haul out to seek a place in the sun on conveniently exposed rocks, sometimes clambering on top of each other in their eagerness.

opaque refuge to contest a place in the sun on conveniently exposed rocks or along the sloping trunks of drowned trees. Herds of impala, nyala, kudu, wildebeest, zebra and giraffe daily trooped in – the crush was heaviest in the mornings between nine and noon. Warthogs were particularly numerous; a sow with 11 piglets all the same age was a regular visitor. Giving birth to 11 babies in one season seemed beyond the capabilities of even the fecund warthog – five or six is the usual limit. Perhaps she had adopted the offspring of a deceased sister.

Shortly after sun-up was the best time for jackals. They hurried in, highstep-

ping and solitary, furtive as thieves, including an abject, hairless one, scabrous with distemper. Blackcollared barbets and bluebilled firefinches splintered the dense air with bright shards of colour. Darting scraps of life – blue and common waxbills – ethereal as butterflies, thronged the water's edge. And every afternoon a lone gymnogene – an infamous nest robber distinguished by its bare vulturine face and nape feathers that protrude in a ruff – put in an appearance, scaring the wits out of all the lesser birds. It first settled in the high bare branches of a killed tree where it meticulously preened itself before coming to

ground and strutting down to drink with the uneasy, feeble-minded arrogance of a *junta supremo*.

Days rolled by in a reassuring, almost unvarying progression. But the air of ordered continuity had no basis in reality where the pan was concerned. It was fully under siege and had already started to shrink and wither away. There had been no winter showers to help sustain it; the whole land was parched and prone. Precursory summer cloudbursts, normal for this time of the year, had not yet materialized. Moreover the horizon was clear – of the longed-for burly purple rainclouds there was no sign.

The sun was intense, glaring – igniting a world of light that was hard to bear. All life seemed drawn into the milling, dust-hazed vortex that had evolved around the few remaining waterpoints. By mid-morning, the hungry herds, their thirst slaked, drifted apathetically away from the pan. Several older animals lingered, as if the effort required to leave was too great or perhaps they were merely aware of the pointlessness of seeking grazing elsewhere. Having come to a standstill, they dropped their heads, hunched their backs and waited.

Mkuzi's mean annual rainfall of 634 millimetres and its semi-arid climate

allow little or no moisture surplus in any season. Consequently it suffers an acute shortage of surface water and during dry periods there remain only two permanent sources for game to drink. With each passing year the Mkuzi River's already unstable flow decreases in volume, due largely to increasing agricultural development upstream. The problem is further exacerbated as the existing network of rainwater pans become shallower owing to siltation caused by the churning herds' trampling and overgrazing of the moisture-retaining, soil-binding vegetation. Topsoil which is broken up and displaced by the erosive action of

Shortly after sun-up is the best time for jackals. They arrive, highstepping and solitary, furtive as thieves, nervously lap their fill then hurry away again. And every afternoon a lone gymnogene puts in an appearance, scaring the wits out of all the lesser birds, first settling in the high bare branches of a dead tree to meticulously preen itself before strutting down to drink with the uneasy, arrogance of a junta supremo.

thousands of hooves is later flushed by the short violent summer downpours into the bed of the pans.

Malibali's receding waters left behind mud rich in trace elements – always a great attraction to diets starved of minerals. Impalas ground down the nuggets between their molars with audible relish, foaming at the mouth as they chewed; a troop of baboons earnestly prospected, carefully brushing their finds clean before eating. Soon their cheek pouches bulged. Dominant males investigated the claims of subordinates and appropriated any worthwhile deposits, with the dispossessed animal raising surprisingly few objections.

Zebras and giraffe were the first to stop using the pan's dwindling water reserves. For such heavy animals there was an ever increasing danger of becoming mired. Impalas nervously circled, reluctant to enter the cloying quagmire which they would have to do if they were to sip the turbid water that remained. Nyala showed less discretion, wading in up to their flanks, gingerly and alternately prising each leg loose with a moist sucking sound. Vervet monkeys skipped lightly from one raised outcrop of dried mud to the next, then having skimmed off sufficient moisture fastidiously wiped any clinging dirt from their hands.

Towards the end only the warthogs

could negotiate the glutinous waterhole without difficulty. Indeed, it had become a pig's paradise and they ploughed into the ooze with obvious delight. Their stocky, short-legged bodies have the buoyancy to slide and the power to trot through the mud at will. Where other animals flounder, warthogs go about their squabbles and other everyday affairs in an element uniquely their own.

The wallowing bodies and churning hooves eventually reduced the pan to the sticky consistency of oatmeal porridge and the stage was set for an act of high drama. As a family group of nyala picked its way through the perimeter sludge an impala ram, approaching from behind and wanting to force a passage suddenly jabbed his horns at a fawn in front. The young animal, pained and alarmed, skittered off to one side, straight into a patch of heavy mud and immediately bogged down. It struggled and plunged in an effort to extricate itself but only sank deeper.

The fawn's frantic commotion startled the other nyalas who galloped clear of the pan and did not stop running until they had reached the safety of the treeline, where they pulled up and stared back, confused as to what had happened. The panicked fawn's wild lunging served only to tire it. Thrashing uncoordinately, it pitched face first into the mud, resurfacing with its nostrils clogged, choking for breath. Then, sunk to its withers, exhausted and badly frightened, it lay gasping. An adolescent impala, made curious by the disturbance, approached for a better look but quickly lost interest and moved on.

Finally the fawn was sufficiently recovered to try again and this time, mercifully and against all my expectations it managed to free itself. Instead of attempting to pull clear as it had earlier, it kicked out with its hindlegs, propelling itself forward like a slalom until, touching firmer ground, it used the last of its strength to make several heaving bounds that brought it to the hard dry bank where it collapsed in a bedraggled heap.

Only when its mother, realizing it was safe, hurried back, did the wobbly youngster rise to its feet and, stretching forward, touch noses with her. Then they both set to licking the fortunate fawn's fur free of the clinging mud.

As the pan congealed the resident terrapins started to slowly abandon it. They hauled themselves away, slowly plodding between stubbled grass tussocks and heat-reflecting rocks, reluctant to leave the cool sanctuary that had served them so well. Ahead lay an arduous, dangerous overland journey to the nearest enduring surface water many kilometres away. It was a journey some of them would not survive. Their deaths would go unremarked for nature has seen to it that though individuals die species and cycles live on.

Malibali's year had come to an end. I stayed on to see it out, watch it shrivel and crack, knowing its passing to be

only temporary. With the first heavy rains it would flourish again, in a dynamic cycle of death and renewal as old as Africa itself.

I had first visited Mkuzi at the height of the previous wet season with its landscape as green as Eire and every depression a sweetwater pool. I had thought then what splendid country it was; flat lowlands for the most part with a greater variety of vegetation types than any other of the Zululand parks.

Mkuzi lies to the east of the Lebombo mountain range at the southern end of the Moçambique plain, between the seasonal Mkuzi and Umsunduzi rivers. In the old days, owing to the prevalence of

As Malibali's water reserves dwindle the churning hooves of the animals reduce it to the sticky consistency of oatmeal porridge. In spite of the danger of becoming mired, a nyala shows little discretion when coming to drink – wading in up to its flanks, then gingerly prising each leg loose with a moist sucking sound.

Panicked zebras pull themselves free of the pan's cloying perimeter. A nyala fawn rests after its frantic struggles to escape the quagmire only served to sink it deeper, while an adolescent impala, made curious by the disturbance, approaches for a better look then quickly moves on. Miraculously, the fawn pulls loose and, trembling with exhaustion, stretches forward to touch noses with its mother.

malaria-bearing anopheles, mosquitos and tsetse, this area was largely spared the slaughter of game visited on other parts of Zululand in the second half of the 19th century. It was very sparsely inhabited and used mainly by various Zulu clans as part of their vast winter hunting grounds. Because of its reputation as a 'white man's grave', hunting by the few Whites prepared to risk an expedition into 'amaTongaland' was limited to two or three winter months each year. Although hunting was intense during these months it made little impact on the teeming herds.

In 1912 Mkuzi was officially proclaimed a game park after enjoying several years unofficial protection from the resident magistrate. In spite of border adjustments that reduced it in size and a conference of farmers in 1931, officials and departments involved with Zululand's nagana problems that resolved that 'Mkuzi Game Reserve be abolished and steps be taken to kill off all the game in a systematic and well organized manner. . .' the park managed to survive. Today Mkuzi's future seems secure but cannot be taken for granted – in the upheavals reshaping contemporary Af-

rica nature conservation has a pitifully low priority.

On that first trip I found the wildlife had taken advantage of the profusion of surface water and rich pasturage provided by the good rains to scatter widely. With all the trees in leaf and the grasses standing tall, visibility from a car cruising the tourist roads was limited to a few metres – it was, I felt, no way to assess the park's potential. In spite of the heat the best way to appreciate Mkuzi at this time of the year was on foot. As it was I had no choice; I wanted to visit Nhlonhlela pan and the sycamore fig forest along the Mkuzi River and the only way to get there was to walk. As my guide I was assigned an aged Zulu game guard, whose name I no longer recall because I always thought of him simply as the 'old man', an affectionate term, or its Zulu equivalent 'madala', his own word when referring to himself.

On our initial outing we set off early to enjoy the short period of daylight before the heat. The fig forest was not far from our starting point at Mantuma tourist camp and we reached it just after sunrise. The trunks and main branches of the monarchial yellow-barked trees were

laden with heavy, branched masses of reddish-yellow figs. A troop of baboons harvesting the fruit howled in dismay on sighting us then quickly and silently came down and melted into the surrounding thickets. Threatened by any predator other than man, baboons make for the safety of trees but fully aware that even in the tallest trees they are vulnerable to firearms, they frantically descend to seek cover on the ground when a human approaches. And the group memory must be long for even where baboons have been protected for years they react this way. A young dilatory male, accidently left behind when the rest of the troop fled, had become marooned at the top of a fig tree by our arrival underneath. The miserable animal, in a state of pure funk, involuntarily (I think) loosed an evil shower of urine and liquid faeces that narrowly missed us. The stink was enough and we hurried on, leaving the wretched creature to swarm down the trunk and hurry after his companions.

Many of the giant figs were flung to the ground and lay strewn haphazardly about, their massive buttressed root systems wrenched loose from the earth and gaping skywards. I later heard that a

hurricane had swept in off the Moçambique channel and, in the short seven minutes it took to traverse the forest, laid waste to so much of it. The devastation was as serious as it looked as sycamore figs are the dominant species of Mkuzi's riverine woodlands and play an important role in retaining the swollen river when periodic flooding brings it down in spate. Without them the torrential waters would burst their banks and inundate low lying areas.

In spite of the showy pre-eminence of the fig and fever trees, the Mkuzi River takes its name from the small, well foliaged lavender tree, *Heteropyxis natalensis* that grows on the rocky cliffs that border parts of its course. The lavender tree was highly regarded by the Zulus who used its strongly aromatic, lavender-smelling

leaves to brew medicinal tea and scent tobacco. Inhaling the steam from a decoction of the roots is even reputed to cure nose-bleeds.

My guide turned out to be a happily garrulous old fellow, animatedly chatting away to me in Zulu, knowing full well I understood hardly a word. I contributed to the charade by grinning and nodding, pretending to be suitably entertained by his anecdotes. I wish now I could have understood him better. In hindsight I recognize that my Zululand experience was subtly diminished by my unfamiliarity with the language. There is a lack of spontaneity in translation that stilts a story, robbing it of its immediacy and ethnic flavour. But time was too pressing to learn more than a smattering of everyday phrases. I was, after all, only

visiting although on a personal level my sojourn there meant much more than that implies. The danger for any stranger making observations in a strange land (and because of my absence since childhood that's what I was) is that only the gross truths may manifest themselves, the undercurrents being too ephemeral to pin down. I hoped that in recognizing the pitfalls I could guard against them.

Turning away from the Mkuzi River we followed the game trail up a slight, rocky gradient set about with tall aloes, their dull grey-green leaves armed along the margins with hard recurved reddish-brown teeth. They were the familiar *Aloe marlothii* and months later during a mild Umfolozi July I would see scores of the same species simultaneously burst into orange flower all around my Tho-

Towards the end only the warthogs are able to negotiate the glutinous waterhole without difficulty. Indeed, it has become a pig's paradise and they plough into the ooze with obvious delight. Wallowing is an important aspect of warthog hygiene and rolling ensures an all-over plastering; the treatment ends with a visit to a popular 'rubbing-post' to relieve a particularly irritating itch.

bothi basecamp. The tiny flowers produce copious nectar and from a hide strategically erected amongst a stand of aloes I could marvel from close quarters at the bustling procession of birds, lizards and insects come to tap the sweet liquid without in any way disturbing them. Several species of sunbirds, the males iridescent as winged jewels, dipped curved bills, long hollow tongues protruding, into the tubular flowers. Non-nectivorous birds were stimulated by the mass blooming to join the feast and flocks of glossy starlings, several blackheaded orioles and a pair of scimitarbilled hoopoes arrived first thing each morning. Later these Mkuzi aloes attract their own excited beneficiaries when in winter their purple buds open.

The trail levelled out then suddenly

dropped away precipitously to a broad body of water edged by pallid spectral fever trees 70 metres below. Without warning I had found myself atop Nhlonhlela hill; the water below was the pan of the same name.

Nhlonhlela hill materialized as abruptly as it did because it is not a hill as such but a steep scarp left standing after the valley below had been gouged out by a prehistoric river. The river not only left behind Nhlonhlela and other pans but also the alluvial deposits in which the present day fig and fever tree forests continue to flourish.

The breakup, 225 million years ago, of the mega-continent Gondwanaland – a great landmass that included Africa, South America, India and Australia – resulted in the Mkuzi area being inundated by the sea. The 'hill' where I stood is composed of calcarious sandstones and mudstones that date back to the lower Cretaceous period 135 million years ago when Africa's shorelines started on their final shaping. All around are fascinating marine fossils that date back to this era and although the hill is not a good source of unflawed fossils there are plenty of broken fragments and blocks of hard matrix with firmly embedded shells. Finally, over many more millions of years, a receding Pleistocene sea's shifting shoreline laid down the series of parallel dunes that extend from where we stood to the present coastline, 60 kilometres away.

From Nhlonhlela we turned west towards the wilderness area, a piece of country not encroached upon by roads or buildings or any other sign that man had been there. The old man led the way through verdant, cicada-singing bush at a steady, unhurried pace, stopping whenever I indicated I wished to take a photograph or investigate some matter that had stirred my interest. He watched with polite, baffled amusement whenever I focussed my macro lens on such arcane subjects as a cicada nymph's abandoned husk or the bleached skeleton of a long dead wildebeest. When I turned the camera on him he stood stoically, staring back with bloodshot rheumy eyes old enough to have seen a way of life very different to the one that followed it.

High overhead a pair of tawny eagles performed the burning dives they use against each other in territorial disputes. A male three-streaked tchagra, fleetingly glimpsed, broke off its shrill, pretty, descending mating trill till we had passed. Our sudden appearance around a bend in the trail startled a crested francolin with four tiny striped chicks at heel. The dismayed hen stood transfixed in the middle of the path, completely at a loss at what to do next. The chicks, with inherent wisdom, clustered together and out of sight while their distracted mother raced up and down the path, calling, fluttering her wings in injury simulation then, when we didn't move, stopped to take cover on the opposite side of the path to her chicks and we quietly went on. As we passed the chicks' hideout I thought how well they had concealed

themselves although the cacophony of cheeps issuing from their grass tussock refuge would immediately have alerted any predator to their presence.

Further on, rust-red shadows shifted in deep green foliage – impalas lightly soaring, defying gravity, followed moments later by a collection of chestnut-coloured nyala ewes and young and a single charcoal ram. Before disappearing the ram pulled up and turned to stare at us; the soft pink linings of his twitching ears absorbed the morning light, as the white chevron between his eyes and the ivory tips to his black, lyre-shaped horns reflected it.

In contrast to the impala, the nyala fled at a heavy gallop, like coursing dogs, landing with a solid thump after each bound. Watching them make their rather clumsy and slow-moving escape I had no trouble accepting the theory popular amongst Zululand's conservationists that nyala, primarily inhabitants of riverine bush and woodland, have been able to extend their range into more open country because of the relative scarcity of large predators which could otherwise easily catch them in the open.

It has also been suggested that, where both species occur, the decline in bushbuck numbers is due to the proliferating and more aggressive nyala besting them in the competition for available browse. Nyala have an added advantage in that being mixed feeders they are not as exclusively dependent on browse as bushbuck but, like impala, benefit from the best grazing in the wet season when grass sprouts afresh and from the short growing tips of woody plants in winter

The sycamore fig forest on the Mkuzi River. The trunk and main branches of these monarchial yellow-barked trees are laden with heavy, branched masses of reddish-yellow figs.

after the grass has dried out and become less palatable for most other animals.

In the past when herbivores were free to migrate as circumstances dictated, they lived an opportunistic existence, continually moving from the dry and withered to the wet and green. Different species, some of whom appear quite similar, used particular parts of the same habitat in different ways, sharing resources in a mutually beneficial feeding sequence. This meant reduced competition between species, the widest possible diversity of the animal community and the harmonious conservation of habitat. The system was flexible enough to weather any of the infrequent, natural disturbances that may have occurred but once horizons became bounded by gameproof fences the succession was thrown out of rhythm. Sedentary herds remained year-round on pastures never intended to support such pressures; densities increased at the same time as ecological niches broke down. With the old processes and balances in disarray direct intraspecific competition for diminishing food resources developed between herbivore species that had previously complemented one another. In Zululand's small parks no animal was as successful in exploiting the new order as was the impala. So prolific did it become, so efficient was it in edging out competitors that parks personnel wryly nicknamed it 'the bush cockroach' – an unkind but not inappropriate epithet.

Impalas are highly adaptable and very flexible in the way in which they make a living. They are specialists in utilizing a wide variety of food plants. Their delicate, pointed muzzles permit them to select new growing and therefore the most nutritious grass shoots in the rainy season and high protein herbs, shrubs and bushes in the dry. This gives them an advantage over other species within the circumscribed habitats of Zululand's present day game parks. The selective removal of green leaves by impala has a detrimental effect on grass production out of all proportion to relative biomass. They are even able to prosper on declining pastures while the land and associated herbivores suffer.

To offset this imbalance in the composition of the herbivore communities (recognized as a root cause of grazing problems) surplus impala, as well as other species, are removed each year from Mkuzi and the Hluhluwe-Umfolozi complex. As many animals as possible are captured to be translocated to other game parks or sold to local landowners who want to establish wildlife on their properties. The Natal Parks Board has led the way in the large-scale capture of surplus animals and by their redistribution served a very important conservation goal.

Where there is no 'live' demand excess animals are shot and sold as carcasses, the revenue supplementing the Parks Board's budget. Ecologists have worked out that Mkuzi could produce a minimum sustained yield of 2 000 impala per annum. This presents a strong economic argument for using country that, like Mkuzi, has infertile soils, is drought prone and without reliable water sources – in short, with poor agricultural potential – to farm wild animals, perhaps in conjunction with cattle ranching. Game cropping produces a harvest just as a maize and sunflower planting does and it has already been conclusively demonstrated how, in many regions of Africa, wildlife could yield several times the profit of domestic livestock.

By mid-day the heat had become oppressive yet not so brutal as I remembered it to have been in Namibia. At Mkuzi the brightness was of a different quality. The sun's rays seemed to be absorbed by the greenness, the lush photosynthesizing vegetation had returned it to the atmosphere steaming yet cooler. Even so, the humidity had taken its toil. I was ready for a break and so was the old man. Even those bred to sun and sky in this land with its jarring excesses of light cherish a shady nooning.

We dropped down beneath a big deeply fissured knobthorn, propped ourselves comfortably against a fallen branch and stretched out. Neither of us had brought food for the lunch break – it was too hot to eat. Instead I swigged a mouthful of tepid isotonic mix from my waterbottle. The old man did not carry a waterbottle but when I offered him mine he declined, making me understand that the more one drinks, the thirstier one becomes. It sounded an interesting theory but I decided against testing its validity – I felt sure my kidneys needed topping up.

A moment later I wondered if the old man's decision had been a wise one; he lay on his side, mouth lolling open, to all intents prostrate with heat. Flies crawled on his face and he let them – a bad sign I thought; then I realized he was only dozing. He had dropped off with the facility of a child, ignoring the heat, the flies and the hard ground, totally giving himself over to rest and recuperation – an enviable talent.

A herd of about 20 wildebeest that we had started from their siesta had settled down again except for an old bull a little apart from the main herd. He appeared particularly put out by our presence, repeating in his nasal voice the same silly plaintive – 'kwang' – over and over again. Nothing else within earshot took any notice, not even other wildebeest but he wasn't in the least discouraged. It was hard enough being a wildebeest, he seemed to suggest, without also having people park on your doorstep as well.

There's no way around it – the wildebeest is a singularly ridiculous creature. They have a look of perpetual surprise on their forlorn flat faces; their well-developed necks and shoulders dwindle away to skinny, half-finished hindquarters. They have spindly legs and a jerky gallop reminiscent of a mechanical wind-up toy. When excited they leap and cavort as if determined to reaffirm their reputation as nature's extroverts. Yet though ungainly and unlovely, wildebeest are by no means unloved and it is their delightfully nutty behaviour that is perhaps their most appealing quality.

Wildebeest bulls are sometimes seen to engage in bizarre antics; Mkuzi, particularly at Msinga and Bube waterholes where herds congregate to drink, is the perfect stage setting for these ham actors. Bucking, spinning, racing around in circles and crazily kicking up their heels like feckless calves is in fact a bull's way of intimidating potential competitors, as well as proclaiming that he is in possession of that piece of ground. If two bulls meet and neither gives way they resort to a 'challenge ritual' that includes sparring, feinting and locking horns in a test of strength. But there are conventions to be observed which inhibit overreaction so that honour is satisfied without incurring injuries.

While the old man slept I lay flat on the ground, and listened to the grasses grow, their seeds fall. A butterfly tickled my arm. I believe I actually grinned with contentment. Always at times like that, at leisure with nothing better to do, I thought how lucky I was to be living that way. I had everything a man could desire and I knew it.

Across my line of vision a mob of drongos, bulbuls and crowned plovers pursued and harried a pied crow commuting from one acacia to the next. From the shelter of its perch the crow answered his tormentors with a loud froggy 'kwahk', as droll and contemptuous as a carefully enunciated obscenity.

I have met with the crow everywhere I've travelled in Africa and always found

him to be an enterprising piratical fellow who states his business in an ill-bred voice that I have a great deal of affection for. In Umfolozi I have seen him circling on high in the company of vultures inspecting a cheetah kill, unrecognizable had he not enthusiastically broadcast his whereabouts by cawing over and over again. Fixed black against the inverted blue bowl of the sky amongst that silent assemblage of calculating vultures, the crow's cries had the ring of triumph of one whose temerity knows no bounds and who has always got away with it.

In Etosha during a period spent at home, I put out at the same hour each morning leftovers of old bread and offcuts of meat for the garden birds to sort through. Before long they came to expect the offerings on a regular basis. Infallibly advised by their internal clocks, they would begin boisterously gathering

shortly before the appointed time. If for any reason I was delayed the crows would strut along the kitchen windowsill, imperiously tapping their bills against the pane, cawing loud reminders – vociferous emissaries from the hungry restless suppliants outside.

After our rest the old man and I started back by a most circuitous route, looking for black rhino. We had already seen several but had had no luck in photographing them. At an early stage in my Zululand odyssey I thought I might have trouble getting the material I wanted on the capricious, thicket-loving black rhino – the docile white I had no qualms about. As it turned out, I need not have worried. In those Zululand parks where they occur, black rhinos are not uncommon, only uncommonly difficult to come up with. The only feasible way to approach without disturbing them is on foot. Naturally, wandering about never far from big game results occasionally in close encounters of the terrifying kind. It is an invigorating price to pay and the unpredictability of this kind of photography had a tonic effect on me.

There are those who would argue that pictures depicting wild animals reacting with fear or aggression to the photographer's presence are unnatural and aesthetically repellant, that the human element is far too intrusive. Maybe so, but it is the confrontation pictures – a group of white rhino formed into a defensive huddle, myopically probing for the source of their alarm; a herd of buffalo, moist muzzles raised to the breeze, curved horns heliographing a primal warning or a charging black rhino bearing down like a runaway tank – that best define the antithetical relationship that exists between man and wild beast and more so today than ever before. As it is most wildlife photographers working in Africa are acutely aware of their role as chroniclers of a dying wilderness.

Going into the bush carrying my photographic paraphernalia across my shoulders put me in mind of the pioneer cameramen at the turn of the century whose classic prints bear witness to a turning point in the continent's history. Working with the slow emulsions and long exposures of a very imperfect medium, they brought back images that are monuments of extraordinary patience and tenacity – still useful qualities in contemporary wildlife photographers. Yet other than a kindred spirit and a shared sense of adventure the differences between photographers slogging through the bush now and then are enormous. Certainly my 35 mm Nikon had little enough in common with Arthur Dugmore's favourite reflex camera, a huge bulky box weighing nearly 8 kilograms without plates. Walking for hours under a hot sun with such a ponderous piece of furniture around his neck is a tribute to any man's stamina.

In 1909 on a safari to Kenya's Olgeri River, Dugmore had his first encounter with rhinos: 'Such a good chance for some close work was just what I had been hoping for and so after waiting until we were sure he was soundly asleep, I changed the telephoto lens for another regular quick one and started forward with utmost care. My companion, with his .450 rifle, was immediately behind me . . . As quietly as possible we stalked the sleeping creature until at 30 yards we were close enough for all practical purposes. My companion stood slightly to one side and I made some noise. Like a flash the big animal was up and without waiting a moment he headed for us with erect tail and nostrils dilated, snorting as he came. It was a splendid sight but not one to linger over. I was watching him on the focussing glass of the camera, and when he seemed as close as it was wise to let him come, I pressed the button and my companion fired as he heard the

shutter drop. The shot struck the beast in the shoulder and fortunately turned him at once. At the point of turning he was exactly 15 yards, but it seemed more like five.' That photograph is a dramatic masterpiece and still one of the best rhino pictures ever taken.

Turning a charging rhino with a well-placed bullet was not one of the options open to me but that afternoon I accidently discovered a method of getting close-ups without exposing myself or my subject to risk of injury. We came on a black rhino cow and her sub-adult calf leisurely browsing on the newly sprouting lilies and acacia seedlings. The old man motioned me to go on while he made himself comfortable in a patch of shade. I skirted downwind of them and as they were now feeding towards me I decided to wait up a tree in the hope that they would remain on course.

Top left. The old man stared back with bloodshot rheumy eyes old enough to have seen a way of life very different from the one that followed it. Left. A cicada nymph's abandoned husk.

An impala ram – the 'bush cockroach'. So successfully have impala adapted to the Zululand parks' disrupted and changing vegetation cover that their numbers have dramatically increased to the detriment of other herbivore species.

I chose a marula – as they come without thorns and therefore are great favourites of mine. Getting myself and the tripod into position proved noisier than I had anticipated however, and removing dry twigs to ensure a clear line of fire meant more noise, which the approaching rhinos heard and reacted to. Nervous curiosity thoroughly aroused, the cow rushed up to investigate, her calf in close rearguard support – a turn of events that couldn't have suited me better. The clicking of the camera kept them keyed up, the cow shuffling forward then distractedly backing away, her stolid armoured head traversing left to right while the calf stared with ferocious intensity in the wrong direction.

When the tension became intolerable the rhinos would turn tail and charge off, only to pull up again without going very far. Then I found I could lure them back with whistles and hisses, carefully coaxing them closer until they were almost directly beneath me.

Months later I was to learn from Richard Emsley that 'calling up' black rhinos (white rhinos won't respond) in this fashion is well known in Umfolozi. As with most things though, Richard had evolved his own peculiar version of rhino hailing. He would throw back his head and cause a crazed high pitched whinny to percolate out the back of his throat. It was a horrible sound, accompanied for maximum effect by grotesquely flared

Bucking, spinning, racing around in circles and crazily kicking up his heels like a feckless calf is the wildebeest bull's way of intimidating potential competitors, as well as proclaiming that he is in possession of that piece of ground. If two bulls meet and neither gives way they resort to a 'challenge ritual' that includes sparring, feinting and locking horns in a test of strength.

nostrils and wild rolling eyes. He was like a man possessed. His blood curdling performance certainly galvanized any rhinos within hearing although they were more likely to rush off in panic than draw nearer which, for all I know, may have suited Richard perfectly well.

Preoccupied as I had been with my photography I hadn't noticed the flocks of solid cumulus billowing up from the south-west. Then as the rhinos moved away for the last time I saw how they looked within the context of their wild and irregular landscape. The whole country was bathed in dramatic storm lighting so that the trees and grasses glowed viridian; the light made the rhinos seem more solid, monolithic, like granite boulders impressed upon and made part of the earth; the eastern sky hung down like a heavy velvet blanket. It was artistic license gone mad and something simply to look at – no photograph could do it justice.

The old man was anxious to be home before the rains came and we hurried away. We were not as far from Mantuma

as I had thought. We got back as the westering sun dipped behind the clouds, firing them brilliantly along the top and drawing a dark line underneath. Our return was only minutes before the storm broke. Standing on the verandah of the reception office we watched pellets of rain ricochet off the courtyard's hard surface and traded grins at our narrow escape. I had had a long, happy day and a successful one. The old man had been more than a guide, he had been a friend.

I didn't get back to Mkuzi until the end of the dry season. Having waited until the Malibali pan had cauterized and blistered, I called on the old man again. I planned a walk along the Mkuzi River – dry at that time of the year except for isolated pools – where it forms the park's western boundary, ostensibly to visit a cave reputed to contain a few weathered examples of rock art. My old guide recognized me at once and asked if this walk was to be as long as the last. I didn't know; the purpose of my hikes is usually less specific than was this one. I prefer to allow events to develop, to fol-

low whatever interesting paths chance happens to put in my way.

Again we started early. We had arranged to meet at the old man's quarters near Mtshopi entrance gate and from there we walked the short distance to the Mkuzi River gorge. The intervening countryside had recently been burnt and there had been no rain since the fire; the land was charred and looked sterile, although it was not. The chalk white ash of a slow burning leadwood lay in stark relief against the blackened earth. Spring fires are set by the park's staff to burn off the grasses top hamper of old unpalatable leaves and culms. If this dead material is not removed it accumulates on top of the new growing points, preventing light from reaching them until the tuft is smothered, becomes moribund and eventually dies. By destroying seedlings and stunting the growth of immature plants, fire also directly inhibits the spread of bush encroachment. It recycles nutrients in the form of ash and reduces the risk of disastrous, uncontrolled fires caused naturally, acci-

dentally or by arson – the latter threat sometimes an expression of resentment towards the park's existence.

The Mkuzi's sandy bed was flanked on either side by towering sandstone cliffs irregularly dotted with aloes and primordial cycads. We did not have far to go to reach the cave which fronted directly onto the river. When in spate it must surely lap the prehistoric home-site's water-shaped front step. A rock cast like a masoned seat and worn smooth by years of wear and human grease, stands near the entrance. The ceiling is blackened by past fires and there is a crude hearth, still used, most likely by local goatherds. On the wall behind the hearth, on a low smooth surface, is a chipped and faded collection of red ochre drawings, representing men and beasts. One scene appears to depict a hunt but the figures are faint and difficult to interpret.

The old man sat on the moulded rock and waited for me. I called his attention to the paintings, thinking he might have an explanation, but he only smiled and nodded without coming over. Perhaps having seen them in the past they bored him but I suspect his careless attitude towards these Khoisan bushmen relics may reflect the contempt in which the little hunters themselves are held even to this day by most Africans.

The cultural chasm separating the cattle-owning, crop-rearing, iron-working folk and pottery-making Bantu-speaking clans that penetrated the Mkuzi area from the north some 500 years ago and the indigenous hunter-gatherer nomads was absolute. The Bantu laid great store by material wealth and despised as impoverished and bestial the Khoisan's whole way of existence. An unknown Zulu is quoted as having said of them: 'The Abatwa are very much smaller people than all small people; they go under the grass and sleep in anthills; they go in the mist; they live in the up country in the rocks . . . Their village is where they kill game; they consume the whole of it, and go away . . .' Made desperate by the invasion of their hunting grounds, the Khoisan fought back with

Scenes at a waterhole. Some animals, like these banded mongoose, are exposed and vulnerable to predation when they come down to drink so they waste no time about it, scurrying off as precipitously as they arrived. Warthogs are more confident in their comings and goings, staying on to indulge in a little socializing that frequently degenerates into arguments, while the yellowbilled egret, far left, and grey heron make their home there, stealthily treading the water in search of fish, frogs and crabs.

Their curiosity aroused, this black rhino cow and calf are keyed up; the cow shuffles forward then distractedly backs away, her stolid armoured head traversing left to right while the calf stares with ferocious intensity in the wrong direction.

poisoned arrows and a hunter's skill and independence in the bush but their situation was hopeless. They waged a protracted war of attrition against enemies that hated them with a hatred bred of fear. They were shown no mercy and very likely expected none. They all perished; only the paintings remain and they are badly defaced and may not survive much longer.

The old man led the way a little further down the river course then picked up a narrow, overgrown game trail that went straight up the vertical wall of the gorge. It proved a murderous climb. As if the steep gradient was not bad enough, the trail soon petered out and we were reduced to crawling much of the way on hands and knees through a tangle of thorn bush and choked thickets across treacherous rocky ground in breathless heat that built up by the minute. At one stage I got badly hung up in an *Acacia senegal* thicket. This foul shrub comes armed with thorns in groups of three, the middle one hooked downwards with

the other two curved upwards, a difficult and painful combination to prise loose. By the time I had unpicked myself blood and sweat were freely flowing; sweat stung my eyes, moisture-seeking flies had free run of my face and I fairly seethed with angry self-pity. When we at last reached the crest I was as physically exhausted as I had been in a long while and the old man was grey with fatigue.

But as my breathing steadied my composure was restored and at first grudgingly then with increasing enthusiasm I conceded that the view from up there was in itself reason enough to have made the climb. Looking east I could see all the way to the jagged outline of forested dunes flanking the Indian Ocean. At my back crowded the looming storied Lebombo mountains, runnelled and worn with age, repository of lost Zulu history and folklore. The surrounding plains looked smooth and faded, cast in their igneous browns and greys like the colours in pottery, except for the green-necklaced blue of Nsumu Pan. I recognized the soft cone of Ndundakazi Hill where exists a disturbed cairn of weather-beaten stones rumoured to be the grave of two 15th century Arab traders. The site is thought to have been used as a staging post before making the dash across the malarial lowlands to rendezvous with dhows hoving to at Maputo, Kosi Bay or St Lucia.

At the opposite edge of my vision a fire belched smoke which I assumed was sugar cane being burnt prior to harvesting. A noisy party of neatly dressed mocking chats scrambled amongst a nearby tumble of boulders while a roving flock of redwinged starlings – the red windows in their wings prominent in flight – swept by. From overhead where whitenecked ravens coursed the thermals came a loud scream followed by a small sonic boom, like the sound of a swooping kestrel, as an alpine swift hurtled across the sky. A grey duiker

doe tip-toed between fire scorched elephant's foot and Bushman's candles to reach a patch of shrubbery missed by the voracious flames.

In a clearing in the woodlands immediately below I watched through binoculars as two nyala rams glided by in re-

In adult nyala the colour difference between male and female pelage is most striking, but occasionally oddities occur. Although young males retain juvenile features for sometime after puberty, this ram has retained its juvenile pelage, similar to that of the adult female, into adulthood. A normally developed young ram is apparently fooled into 'testing' a so called 'cryptorchid' ram believing it to be female.

Another abnormality. Impala ewes should be hornless but this horned female, left, proves a rare exception. The horns add to her delicate beauty, appearing almost as though she were wearing a coronet.

verse parallel to each other, their necks arched and white dorsal crests raised, in an elegant, highly stylized, slow motion challenge ritual. As tension increased their walk became slower and they half raised their tails to display fluffy white undertufts. Their heads were held low,

Nyala rams glide by in reverse parallel, their necks arched, white dorsal crests raised and tails flared, in an elegant highly stylized slow motion challenge ritual.

Right. On the road from Mkuzi to Ndumu a Zulu kraal, with Itshaneni, the Ghost Mountain of Rider Haggard fame, looming in the background. Many older Zulus still refuse to set foot on the mountain, a battlefield between two Zulu factions in the early part of this century and believed by some to possess the spirits of the many killed in the clash. An area where corpses are left unburied, and not in graves according to tradition, is regarded as hallowed ground and treated with the respect accorded a graveyard.

in line with their bodies, with their horns pointing forward. Neither animal gave way and they stopped walking, only moving to keep their striking profiles orientated towards each other. In this 'lateral presentation' the area of an adult male's silhouette is increased by as much as 40 per cent by a long fringe of hair on each side of his belly and hind legs together with the erectile ridge of white hair running along his spine. Moreover his torso appears to be laterally compressed so that in cross-section he is more elliptical than oval.

The rams abruptly broke off displaying and busied themselves with displacement grooming, then carefully moved apart. The outcome was inconclusive but other contests that I have witnessed, when one animal was obviously bigger than his opponent, size always prevailed.

Dominance displays such as this have evolved to minimize fighting and the risk of sustaining injuries either fatal or serious enough to leave an animal vulnerable to predation. Young nyala males that lock horns in trials of strength come to realize that opponents larger than themselves are likely to win any physical encounter. As they get older, stronger and potentially more dangerous so challenge displays replace sparring as a means of achieving dominance. Although horns play a role in the ritual, it is not horn size but body size and those features that emphasize it decide the outcome. The dominant rams that monopolize oestrous females and so pass on their genes have ensured a selection towards large male size and strategically situated crests and fringes of hair. The consequence of all this evolutionary en-

gineering is a creature not only wonderfully functional but also one of the most beautiful in Africa.

A troop of vervet monkeys played on the forest perimeter where it gave way to the grasscap we rested on. The vervets scampered and quarrelled, groomed and foraged, sometimes remembering to harangue us but without conviction. I watched them past the bulk of the old man who sat a little ahead of me. He too was looking towards the vervets but I wondered if he really saw them. He had lived all his life with such scenes and doubtless had domestic worries to occupy his mind. Anyway, I had been told on more than one occasion (by so-called 'experts') that Africans have no aesthetic appreciation of wildlife. Then he turned to me and on his face was a smile of pure delight. He was as charmed by the vervets

as I. His smile gave eloquent emphasis to my growing awareness that in spite of the cruel and absurd legislation that seeks to drive the races apart, each has more in common with the other than they care to admit. Surrounded by sun and space and the murmur of life all around it seemed not only morally right but correct within the natural order that the disparate cultural and ethnic poles setting the old man and I apart were of far less importance than our shared humanity and mutual love and appreciation of the Earth that sustained us.

This view from the top of the Mkuzi River gorge is the best in the district although the lookout from Itshaneni – the Ghost Mountain of Rider Haggard fame – is better known. Ghost Mountain was originally part of Mkuzi and there is talk of trying to get it re-included but the

Ndumu Game Reserve is best known for its birdlife and plays host to an astonishing 393 species. A series of shallow lakes or pans lying adjacent to the rivers hold water throughout the year.

The end is not far off for this cattle egret chick, below, recently fallen from its nest; however, the cries of the trumpeter hornbill heralds new life with a variety of cat-calls, wails, screams and brays.

Crested guineafowl, distinguished from their crowned cousins by a graceful topknot of curling black feathers, waddle forth purposefully while male saddlebill storks preen. Although the male is distinguished by his bright yellow wattles both sexes have a livid medallion of bare flesh on their breasts.

prospects are not good. As I had planned to pass right by the mountain a few days later on my way to Ndumu Game Reserve, I had arranged with the farmer whose property it bordered to climb to its summit.

Unlike the gorge, the ascent to Gaza – one of the Itshaneni's twin peaks – was steep but not difficult. Rider Haggard wrote 'King Solomon's Mines' while posted as stationmaster to Mkuze village and when I looked south towards Hluhluwe I could see in the distance the two gently rounded, paired hills thought to have inspired the landmark Sheba's Breasts that, in the book, point the way to the hidden mines.

Ghost Mountain takes its name from the Zulu belief that it is possessed by the spirits of the many people killed there in a clash between two Zulu factions in the early part of this century. Zulu religion was based on family spirit worship. Although the permanent home of spirits is the grave, a battlefield where the corpses were left unburied is regarded as hallowed ground and treated with the respect and awe accorded a graveyard. Many older Zulus still refuse to set foot on the mountain. Until quite recently it was possible to discover relics of the battle in the form of skulls, spearheads and at least one muzzle-loader that was found by a local white farmer.

The road to Ndumu leads over the wall of the controversial Jozini dam then north to the Pongolo floodplain. The large (10 000 hectares) and highly productive floodplain is formed by the Pongolo River's seasonal run-off overflowing its banks and flooding the surrounding land. In so doing it deposits part of its nutrient rich silt load and provides natural irrigation. This oasis in northern Zululand's otherwise semi-arid Ingwavuma district has been jeopardized over the last decade by badly timed releases of water from the Jozini dam that

Nyamiti pan teems with life – and death: the dabchick repeatedly dunks a dragonfly in order to drown it before swallowing it whole; a hippo's head makes a convenient perch for a jacana in search of water insects; a stilt warily negotiates between basking crocodiles, while a pair of Egyptian geese shepherd their goslings out of harm's way.

have had a profound effect on the floodplain's ecology. Careless releases have unseasonally flooded the crops of tribes people dependent on the Pongolo River and its floodplain for their livelihood. Withholding water artificially caused the greatest drought in living memory, resulting in an outbreak of typhoid and seriously harming fish populations. The viability of the floodplain as an ecosystem depends on intelligently planned future water releases, correctly timed and of appropriate magnitude.

Floodplains rank with coral reefs and estuaries as the world's most productive natural ecosystems. Those sections of the lowlying grass and sedge-dominated Usutu and Pongolo floodplains within Ndumu Game Reserve spectacularly demonstrate the number and variety of wild creatures this habitat can support. A series of shallow lakes or floodplain pans lying adjacent to the rivers hold water throughout the year and in themselves represent differing minor ecosystems; they may have fresh water or saline, be large or small, have muddy banks or be fringed by dense reedbeds. Some have little aquatic vegetation; others are thickly covered with waterlilies and other free-floating or rooted floating plants; yet others have extensive submerged aquatic plant communities. These perennial pans provide a refuge for fish during the dry winter season when flow in the rivers is minimal. Many species of birds are attracted to their resources. Ndumu's large reedbeds form one of only two known openbill stork breeding sites in South Africa.

These wetlands are important winter feeding grounds for whitefaced duck, Egyptian geese, spurwing geese, redbilled teal and other waterfowl feeding on curly pondweed. The over-wintering flocks may reach a density of 100 birds per hectare, a reflection of the floodplain's high level of productivity.

Ndumu lies on Zululand's northern border with Moçambique and was proclaimed in April 1924 primarily as a hippo sanctuary. Today it is one of the last game reservoirs in northern Zululand. Towards the end of the last century when hides were in great demand and realized good prices, winter hunting parties of Transvaal Boers decimated the buffalo, eland and kudu herds – by all accounts the three most common big game species at the time. In the wake of the devastating rinderpest epidemic of 1897/98, followed in the late 1930s and early 1940s by the destruction of animal populations by white biltong hunters and the tsetse game elimination campaigns, buffalo and eland disappeared altogether. Since then what little remained outside Ndumu was removed by hunting and snaring tribesmen – an occupation at which they were past masters.

Ndumu is best known for its birdlife. In spite of its small size – 10 117 hectares – it plays host to an astonishing 393 different species, many of them East African forms at the southern limit of their range. Ndumu's great diversity of bird species can be attributed to its remarkable array of ecosystems within an ecosystem. They range from the prolific floodplains through tall tree savannas, dense acacia thickets, riverine and swamp forests to dry tropical forests. Where different vegetation types form such a mosaic, a greater variety and number of birds and mammals can exist than would otherwise be the case.

Towards sunset I drove down to the incomparable Nyamiti pan on the Pongolo floodplain. In the old days the local Tembe people were in the habit of sacrificing virgins on appropriate occasions to Nyamiti's resident crocodiles. Although the custom is no longer practised, and given that crocodiles live for over a century, it seems quite feasible that some of the older gourmets patrolling the pan that evening once feasted on that most exclusive of delicacies.

As I approached through the screening trees, Nyamiti announced itself in

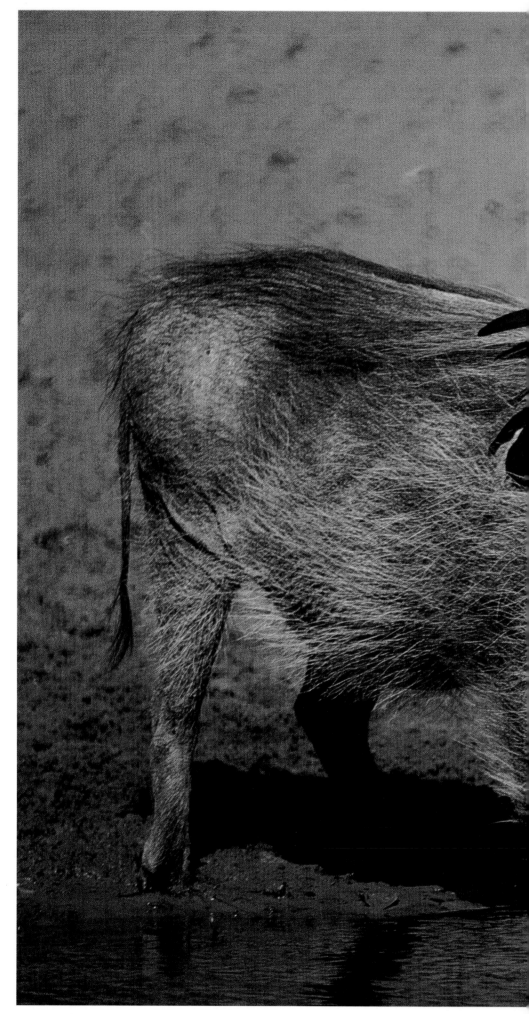

the form of a grey heron, tiny in the distance, standing like a figurine at the edge of a piece of glassy water. Then, after I had gone beyond the trees an harmonious coming together of water, forest and wildlife was revealed, imposing its beauty boldly and irresistably. The still shallow water reflected a dying sun that kindled early spring clouds into brief priceless colours and shades. Fresh pink lines of late feeding flamingos cracked the mirror and a string of cattle egrets in laboured flight flared against the forests' dark backdrop. The long-stemmed silhouettes of goliath herons and yellow-billed storks; the serrated back and long ridged tail of a partly submerged crocodile; the foreshore was littered with waterfowl – spoonbills, whitefaced and knobbilled ducks, cackling Hottentot teal, spurwing and Egyptian geese; the water's edge teemed with stilts and sandpipers, avidly feeding before nightfall. A motionless group of hippos in the centre of the pan shone like wet rocks in the evening light, their grunts, like the turgid laughter of old men enjoying a ribald joke, is the loudest sound there is.

I walked to the last stand of fever trees abutting the beach. A grass owl flew across the space of sky between the branches, moving as silently as a fish. A covey of handsome, forest-dwelling crested guineafowl – distinguished from their cackling crowned cousins by a graceful topknot of curling black feathers – exploded into flight with rattling alarm calls. This is the finest hour – night darkening over, waiting and listening for day to be gone and the arrival of twittering sandgrouse whirring to water.

The raucous pied crow states his business.

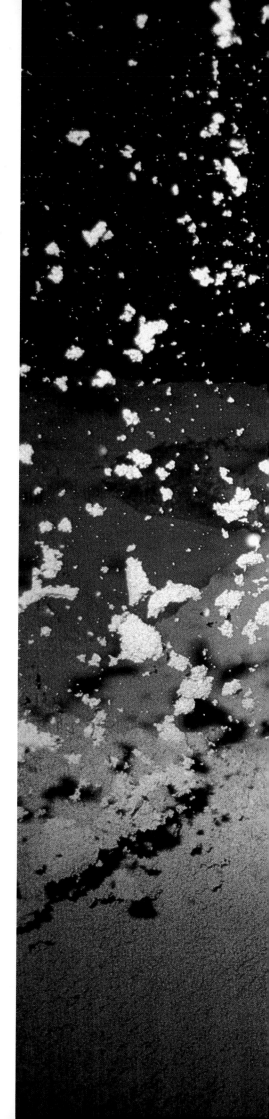

The circle closed with mysterious tracks on a lonely Tongaland beach; like the unbroken tread of an earth-moving machine, they led from the breakers to a depression above the highwater line, then turned and went back into the sea. It was the mark of a loggerhead turtle that had come ashore the previous night to nest, though had I not been there at that particular time of the year specifically to see the marine turtles for myself, I might never have guessed what had made those enigmatic prints.

The beach is called Bhanga Nek. It forms the narrow landbridge separating Kosi Bay from the Indian Ocean and is only a few kilometres south of Ponta do Ouro across the border in Moçambique. For two decades now the Natal Parks Board has maintained an outpost there where a survey team studies and protects the female loggerhead and leatherback turtles that haul out at night during the summer months to excavate a nest and lay their six score eggs in the sand.

Five species of sea turtles – the green, hawksbill, olive ridley, loggerhead and leatherback – occur in these south-east African waters but only the latter two nest at Bhanga Nek. This wild splendid stretch of Tongaland coastline, where narrow beaches abut steep thicketed dunes, forms the most southerly and one of the largest turtle nesting sites on the entire east coast of Africa. Presently more than 80 leatherback and up to 500 loggerhead females every year swim in total hundreds of thousands of kilometres through dangerous waters to the safe nesting offered by these beaches. Yet in 1966, when the conservation programme started, only five leatherbacks and some 200 loggerheads were counted in the whole five-month season. It was not until the protection of the Tongaland shores was guaranteed by Natal Parks that their populations started to recover.

The survey team comprises the Parks Board officer-in-charge, two students from Natal University in Pietermaritzburg and two rangers detached from KwaZulu Conservation Division as well as several locally hired Thonga tribesmen. The study area stretches from the estuary at Kosi Bay in the north to south of Mabibi – a distance of 56 kilometres, the entire length of which is patrolled every night during the nesting season.

TRACKS IN THE SAND

'. . . perhaps most incredible of all, these endangered reptiles that have survived almost unchanged for 100 million years may well have returned to this area to perpetuate their species for almost as long as that.'

Under a great floating moon I joined district ranger Eddie Harris as he made his rounds in a low-slung beachbuggy.

Harris drove fast – he had to, there was a long way to go and a lot to do – but he navigated the shore with the watchfulness of one who knew that the way ahead was treacherous and changeable from day to day. The motion of the waves irregularly smothered then exposed rocks so that a smooth stretch of sand one night could become a sump-gutting hazard the next. That night a thickly woven carpet of bluebottles left stranded by a retreating tide lightly popped under the buggy's passage in sibilant counterpoint to the mutter of the ocean. Companies of ghost crabs, pincers held high, retreated sideways in close-column to the sheltering sea. Sanderlings and sandplovers flared briefly in the headlights, whirling straight up into the darkness like lost souls departing.

Eddie was slightly strung out by the long wearying hours the job required at that particular time of year, and knew it. 'If I sometimes act irritable,' he said, 'it's because I don't get enough sleep. Sleeping during the day isn't a working proposition – too many other problems keep cropping up.'

Yet he seemed pleased enough to be showing off his protectorate and displayed none of the hardbitten exclusivity or proprietary air that lies just below the bluff bonhomie of many wildlife officials. He spoke with quiet pride and real enthusiasm about what had been achieved there. 'We call this spot the graveyard,' he said of a local landmark where in 1963 a fisherman came upon a pile of turtle carapaces abandoned by resident tribesmen after they had slaughtered nesting females for their red meat; having earlier ripped their ovaries open for unripe eggs. That discovery alerted the Natal Parks Board to the turtle's plight and initiated the conservation effort that continues to this day.

The survey team records the size and related data of all turtles encountered and each has a small monel metal tag firmly clinched into a foreflipper. When the hatchlings emerge the team notches out a piece of its carapace – a different notch site is used for each year's crop. During the course of the 81/82 season – when I visited Bhanga Nek – some 5 600 hatchlings were painstakingly marked.

In the spume-bright wash zone we saw a female loggerhead lying, gathering her strength for the gruelling task ahead. She was wary, alert to danger. Eddie switched off and we waited. Finally, satisfied, the turtle started forward, laboriously dragging herself along on her flippers. She stopped frequently to rest and look around; her beaked inelegant head arcing through its limited radius with the purposefulness of a gun turret. In this attitude she looked like an amphibious tank; there was an aura of indestructibility about her. But nothing could be further from the truth; she was seriously at risk when she came ashore – out of her element and pathetically vulnerable.

The skin of her neck and body, where not protected by shell, was brownish yellow, soft and wrinkled. Her reddish-brown carapace was colonized by six or seven barnacles, another alongside her left eye. One of her shell's rear lateral shields had been gouged in a long past high-sea drama. Glands adjacent to her eyes excreted salt in liquid form that, clogged with beach sand, drooled like forlorn webs of saliva to the ground. She appeared to be weeping and her distressed mien was compounded by an oc-

Each summer about 80 leatherback turtles (far left) and up to 400 smaller loggerheads (left) come ashore at night to nest. Gravid females first excavate a 45 centimetre egg-cavity before laying 120 soft-shelled eggs. Between 55 to 65 days after the eggs are laid, the hatchlings cut their way out using an egg tooth on the end of their beaks and scrabble at the walls and roof of the chamber to free themselves. If they reach the surface during the day they are inhibited from further movement by the heat of the sand and wait until the temperature drops before bursting out and heading for the surf. Once in the water they swim steadily for days to the open sea. Once there, life is extremely hazardous with only one or two from every thousand reaching maturity.

casional deep sigh. The sense of awe and mystery that I felt for this lone representative of an extremely ancient order of reptiles as she emerged from the waves was replaced on closer contact with an unfamiliar surge of protective tenderness – she was so achingly defenceless.

Once she was well above the high-water mark she began casting about for a suitable nest site. Now and then she would thrust her beak into the sand, testing its consistency and odour. Having selected a spot she began digging a body cavity with her foreflippers – and throwing sand backward until she had

excavated a depression level with the top of her carapace. Then, with her hind flippers, she scooped out a flask-shaped egg-cavity about 450 millimetres deep and, having rested awhile, began laying. We drew closer; at that stage her hormones controlled her every move and she was quite unaware of extraneous events.

Delivering in bursts of one to four at a time, the turtle dropped approximately 120 white, spherical, soft-shelled eggs then delicately filled the hole. She pressed and kneaded the sand until it was hard packed, then disguised the site by ruffling the surface with her foreflip-

pers. All that was left was the heaving return journey across the beach. By the time she slid into the safety of the waves she was utterly exhausted.

Loggerheads return up to five times during a season to lay an average of some 600 eggs at 15-day intervals. Periods of absence from the nesting beaches vary but tagging has shown that a female is capable of coming back as often as six different seasons over 18 years, producing 3 600 eggs in her lifetime. Leatherbacks lay up to 1 000 billiard ball-sized eggs per season but probably return no more than three times in their lives.

Loggerhead hatchlings cut their way out of the egg after 55 to 65 days (leatherbacks take a little longer) using an egg tooth on the end of their beaks. I returned to Bhanga Nek two months later over the full moon period in early February to see the 30 millimetre hatchlings struggle to the surface and make their nocturnal dash to the Indian Ocean. Once in the water they swam steadily for several days, then were swept along by the Agulhas current. Notched hatchlings less than 50 millimetres long have been found 1 600 kilometres from their point of departure. But life in the open sea is extremely hazardous for the little creatures and it has been estimated that only one or two from every thousand, reaches maturity. Those that survive drift for up to three years on the Indian Ocean's great gyral currents, feeding on floating organisms such as bluebottles and purple storm snails. Then, as young adults, they return to Bhanga Nek or very near it. Converging loggerheads are drawn from a 4 700 kilometre-long sweep of the African east coast – from Zanzibar in the north to Cape Agulhas on the continent's southern tip. And, perhaps most incredible of all, these endangered reptiles that have survived almost unchanged for 100 million years may well have returned to this area to perpetuate their species for almost as long as that.

As we met up with the two-man foot patrols responsible for a particular section of the beach, Eddie collated their data. The last team comprised two old reprobates, one of whom was called Five, a name that hardly applied to his left hand from which the forefinger was missing – snapped off years before by an indignant turtle he was attempting to restrain and measure while he himself was suffering from the effects of lala palm cider. He looked in pretty poor shape that night – one eye was closed and the side of his mouth broken. Eddie jocularly asked him in Zulu – 'What happened, Five, did your wife beat you up?' The question sent Five's companion off into peals of helpless laughter, though Five could only manage a small unhappy smile. He fidgeted embarrassedly, then glumly nodded 'Yebo' – yes. This was too much for his companion who had tried to politely suppress his laughter but then went completely out of control.

His maniacal whoops set Eddie and I off and finally Five joined in, shaking his head in delighted despair, forgetting his pain, snorting and cackling till tears ran down his cheeks.

The following morning Eddie Harris drove south along the beach and dropped me off at a cycad stand I wanted to look at, then continued on to a high wavecut headland called Black Rock. He was escorting a visiting herpetologist in search of a small diurnal lizard vividly named Bouton's snake-eyed skink, which in Tongaland lives only on Black Rock and in Africa reaches its southern limit there. For Harris it meant more missed sleep but he went without complaint and was even jovial.

Because of the warmth I was only wearing a pair of swimming trunks and in the climb up the tall, overgrown dune, stinging nettles scalded my unprotected legs and torso with the intense, precise pain of a small flame. I tried to ward them off with a dead branch and managed to keep going until I reached the cycads, which promptly rewarded my determination by spearing me with their spine-tipped leaflets.

My interest in this particular stand of cycads – *Encephalartos ferox* – had as much to do with the numbers that occurred here as in the plants themselves. This ancient, palm-like order of cycads is the most primitive of all the seed-producing plants. It is the connecting link between the spore-producing ferns that evolved nearly 400 million years ago and the later flowering plants that fanned across the globe in the Cretaceous period, a fascinating discovery.

Cycads flourished between 300 and 200 million years ago but are now slowly dying out and those that survive today represent only a remnant of this once dominant group. They are amongst the most long-lived plants and these specimens have survived for at least 500, perhaps a thousand years – silent, unassuming sentinels when the first Portuguese explorers sailed this coast.

From the top of the dune, framed by a matching pair of wild bananas, white beaches and blue water filled the eye. At

that point I was too far south to see Kosi Bay to the landward, but at Bhanga Nek we were separated by only 250 metres of sand dune from Lake Nhlange, the largest cell in Kosi's estuary-linked system of four inter-dependent lakes. Before coming over here I had toured much of it by outboard and found it still remarkably untouched, though if the often mooted plan to develop it as a harbour ever eventuates its despoilation will be irrevocable and indeed tragic.

I travelled with two ornithologists, to whom Kosi represented the last leg of a bird survey covering the entire South African coastline. Thanks to them I had several species pointed out to me that I might otherwise have overlooked. Slowly cruising the narrow reed-lined channel joining lakes Nhlange and Sifungwe I was introduced to brownthroated weavers plaiting intricate nests that bobbed gently as the reeds from which they hung trembled in our bow wave. This small, short-tailed weaver is listed in my Roberts as 'very little recorded' and represented a 'life bird' (as they are known to the bird fraternity) for me – the first of their species I had ever seen.

Young yellow crocodiles slipped into the water at our approach and in the open lake phlegmatic hippos, submerged except for their heads, silently watched us pass. In the tidal waters up to the estuary mouth we skirted many of the traditional palisade fish traps built by tribesmen to ensnare marine fish such as grunter and mullet returning to the sea as adults, having entered the estuary seeking food and shelter when they were young. The 18 kilometre-long Kosi system runs roughly parallel to the coastline and there at the northern seaward end is an estuarine basin where fresh and salt water mingle, creating nursery grounds for marine fish.

Going south through the necklace of lakes the water became progressively less saline until we reached, in the afternoon, the fresh, peat-stained aptly named Lake Amanzimnyama, meaning black waters. Giant raffia palms lined the lake's edge and I was thrilled to see a palmnut vulture (another first) sitting in the crown of one. Described in Aves' SA Red Data Book as a 'peripheral and vulnerable resident' it is passionately fond of the husk and fleshy outer-covering of the nuts of these raffia palms and is never found far from them. This handsome vulture that looks like an eagle is one of South Africa's rarest breeding birds. An aerial census carried out in 1982 suggests that the entire population may consist of only six pairs.

The primordial scenes that greeted us on entering the lake's feeder, the Sihadhla River, were straight out of the 'African Queen'. Luxuriant swamp forests overhung the water's edge; its huge trees towered up out of fetid under-stories, raising lofty sunlit crowns. The afternoon heat that day was drawn into the deep fecund green of the place and to the nostrils came the pungence of mouldering leaves, the damp humus smell of sub-tropical forests. A flash of discordant colour and I had my first clear sighting of the beautiful red and green plumed Nerina trogon named by the 18th century naturalist François Levaillant after a Hottentot girl whose beauty he greatly admired. We were in the haunts of the fishing owl and hoped to see this covert, little-known raptor. It spends its days roosting in tall trees and if disturbed flaps off noisily, but we went unrewarded. At night, when hunting, the owl perches on a branch over the river until it sights a fish and – wings spread, eyes closed, its featherless legs and sharp-taloned feet extended – executes a spectacular splash-down, seizes its prey and takes it to shore. It is a performance I've yet to see.

Then as now I was struck by the astonishing diversity of life forms, the

A hermit crab abroad in the late afternoon.

Left: Two members of the turtle survey team which includes Five, whose forefinger was snapped off years ago by an indignant turtle he was attempting to restrain and measure.

In Kosi Bay's shallow sandy estuary Thonga tribesmen have for centuries built ingenious fish kraals to trap grunter, mullet and other marine fishes returning to the sea. The principle on which the kraal works is simple but efficient: straight branches driven into the sand to form a circle two metres in diameter act as a 'guide-fence'; inside the circle a constricted valve, through which fish can enter but not easily escape, is fastened on to the funnel of the guide fence. Live fish are then speared in the water – an easy to harvest source of protein for an avian fisherman such as this greenbacked heron.

sheer overwhelming biological wealth of the place. From the off-shore coral reefs with their 1 200 recorded fish species to Kosi's tapestry of interlinked habitats, this small area supports a web of life that confounds in its intricacy.

Walking back from the cycad stand I found strewn amidst the detritus of seaweed and shells beached along the high-tide line many marble-sized remnants of rendered jellyfish. Adult leatherback turtles feed almost exclusively on jellyfish and it pleased me to think these glassine bits and pieces to be crumbs from the meals of gravid females lying off the coast.

Further along I came upon a green bush snake, washed bright emerald by the play of the tide. Our surprise was mutual and I detoured around it – to leave it in peace where I found it, so removed from its normal environment.

At an extensive rocky outcrop I had my first encounter with Man since climbing the dune. While their menfolk angle with crude tackle in the tidal pools, Thonga women take advantage of the spring low tide to scour the exposed rocks in search of mussels, limpets and other shellfish. In this wild, undeveloped corner the tribes people still live off the land to a remarkable degree. Their rural economy and very survival is dependent on an intimate knowledge of the flora and fauna in their particular area. Natural resources provide food, medicine, utensils, clothing and fuel. But overpopulation, here as everywhere else, places intolerable strains on nature's ability to meet the demands.

In the past these shellfish clusters were able to maintain a recolonization

144

rate more than or equal to the take-off by tribal communities whose numbers were limited by malaria and sleeping sickness. With the eradication of the killer anopheles mosquito and tsetse fly the human population has surged until today all the rocky outcrops together cannot support the continued stripping. In an attempt to contain the damage it is now prohibited to hack off entire rock overhangs to get at inaccessible or submerged shellfish. Research is currently in progress to monitor the legal harvest which may well result in recommendations for further limitations such as rotating and resting outcrops, although already the gatherers complain there is not enough to go around.

As I went on my way small parties of plump-breasted, bustling, white-fronted sandplovers scurried before me. Migrant whimbrels, having come south to avoid the European winter, got up in alarm at my approach and rendered rippling seven-syllabled cries; a rare osprey passed overhead.

The beach was deserted except for a lone Thonga girl chasing down supper in the form of ghost crabs that she stuffed into a basket woven from lala palm fronds. She broke off collection to greet me with a smile so wide and easy I was made to feel genuinely welcome. Her midriff was prettily decorated with diamond patterned cicatricing – the tradi-

tional raised-flesh scarification that is now dying out, even in these remote parts. When I gestured towards the basket she briskly opened it to reveal the contents churning with crabs and sea lice. Seen in that empty immensity, her way of life seemed miraculously uncomplicated and satisfying. I wished for both our sakes it could continue like that, although I knew very well it could not.

Tongaland (sometimes called Maputaland) took its name from the Thonga people although it was a name foreign to themselves. It was, at the time, a derogatory term applied indiscriminately by the Zulus to everybody living north-east of them who remotely appeared to fall by custom or language into the Moçambiquan tribal groups.

Tongaland today is bounded to the west by the Lebombo mountains, to the south by the Mkuzi River, by the Indian Ocean to the east, and to the north by Moçambique – an area of approximately 8 000 square kilometres. It has always been a hard country. 'In what is called the Amatonga country,' David Leslie wrote in his book on the Zulus and Amatongas in the 1870s, '. . . the decayed vegetable matter and stagnant swamps are so great, that it is death to any European to venture there. Miles upon miles of flat country; in fact, one great rich swamp, covered with game, is there inhabited by a people civilized in compari-

son with their neighbours, the Zulus; but where death or disease is sure to attack any white man who enters.'

The Thongas originate mainly from a northern migrant group of Karangas who migrated into the region in the 16th century, absorbing the resident Lala and Malangeni Nguni groups they encountered. After the boundary decision in 1875 which established the present frontier with Moçambique, the various Thonga clans found themselves artificially separated. They all belonged to the Shangane-Ndau-Karanga language group which is quite different from Zulu. During the 19th century however, Zulu invasions and the migration of exiles fleeing Chaka had a profound impact on Thonga society with the result that today two languages are spoken – Zulu by the men and Thonga by the more conservative women who cling to their ethnic roots. This bilingualism has meant dual names or two versions being used for everything, even place names.

Driving the rough road inland from Kosi the sound of my engine brought groups of people waiting at crudely-lettered bus stops to their feet. On seeing it was not their bus they dropped down again into the long grass, amidst litter old and recent. They stared with closed patient faces as I passed, neither hostile nor friendly. Most were dressed in rag-

tag trading store clothing, with an occasional stiffly creased uniform and one whose outsize dark glasses and sharp leatherette slouch cap proclaimed him an outspoken convert to the new Africa. Wherever I stopped children gathered around with bold-eyed, wide-open curiosity and all the time in the world to indulge it.

Terra dos Fumo – the Land of Smoke – was the name given by the early Portuguese navigators to this southern end of the Moçambique plain where columns of smoke from frequently burnt grasslands identified it to passing ships. Yet in spite of fire, cultivation and the introduction of domestic stock, the region has managed till now to maintain a reasonable measure of its ecological diversity due to low population densities. But what of the future? Unhappily it has already been necessary in the heavily populated coastal zone for three-quarters of all adult males to work in city or industrial jobs because the leached, overworked soil is unable to support so many people.

It was some months later, but not far as the crow flies from the beaches where the turtles haul out, that I stared down at an altogether different set of tracks – the familiar, round, wrinkled pad of a bull elephant, set deep in the yielding sands of the Sihangwane forest. Nothing could have seemed more natural than elephant spoor in that silent, arid sand forest with its towering marulas and pod mahoganies. Indeed, elephants have visited these parts over the ages for the abundance of fruit produced by its trees and shrubs during the summer months, although otherwise it would not be preferred habitat as the poor, leached soils support only coarse sour herbage of extremely low nutritive value. The only fertility lies in the top 200-millimetre layer of finely divided humus and ash deposited by centuries of fires. That factor, together with the waterless nature of the country, has, till now, meant a sparse human population but in the current scramble for land, encroachment is occurring and pressures are building.

Sihangwane's free-ranging elephants belong to the same breeding population as those in the Maputo Elephant Reserve in adjacent Moçambique; they represent the last elephants in Moçambique south of the Limpopo and the only survivors in

Zululand. The herds have always migrated back and forth between the two areas but in recent years the number concentrating in Sihangwane has increased considerably. This large influx is made up of refugees from Maputo Reserve where up to 10 000 villagers have settled and as a consequence, poaching on a massive scale is the order of the day. Many of the persecuted elephants, escaping the ensuing massacre, fled south and there ran up against impoverished subsistence farmers. During the December-to-April crop season some of the elephants took to supplementing their diet by raiding maize and groundnut patches of resident Thonga cultivators. So, in the struggle for diminishing resources the stage was set for one of the classic confrontations that is invariably occuring throughout Africa today: embattled elephants, crowded and cornered, making a last stand against peasant farmers whose hardscrabble existence is further undermined by the depredations of the world's largest land mammal.

In 1981 the push between Tongaland's elephants and pastoralists came to shove. Single bulls and bachelor groups, often covering great distances by night, raided crops and sometimes overturned the huts of terrified villagers. Game scouts of KwaZulu's Nature Conservation Division, charged with maintaining law and order, found themselves hopelessly over-extended. Complaints poured in. Why, the irate farmers demanded – not unreasonably – did authorities put the welfare of elephants before people? What use were elephants anyway?

Happily, KwaZulu's plans are already well advanced for the establishment of the Tembe Elephant Reserve with one of its first priorities being the erection of an elephant-proof fence to separate the protagonists. Herb Bourn, head of the division, outlined his department's policies: 'Our philosophy is that parks musn't be seen as separate from regional development. It is no longer enough to simply pass laws prohibiting people from poaching, clearing forests for food and agriculture – we've got to provide alternative sources of food and finance. We are a conservation body but we cannot isolate ourselves from rural interests and people.'

He continued, 'We decided in the beginning to sell conservation from a prac-

Scenes from the swamp forest are straight out of the 'African Queen'. With grim patience, a night adder waits for its poison to take effect on a fear-bloated frog it grips in its fangs. A snake can eat up to a quarter of its own weight in one sitting – a human would have to be a glutton to manage five per cent. Through a complicated system of articulations and elastic ligaments it can open its jaws four times as wide as a human and by lubricating its prey with saliva it painstakingly ingests it. Resembling a rollercoaster (left) a boomslang's camouflaged skin dips and dives over the branches while a locust sets about destroying the foliage.

tical point of view – to set aesthetics aside – but in our dealings with tribal leaders we found them very responsive to both. So aesthetics are important.'

That importance was brought home to me soon after arriving at Sihangwane store, where Nature Conservation has its district headquarters. The amiable training NCO, Andries Malwane, invited me to join him on a courtesy call to one of the more prosperous local farmers. Richard Mhlongo, a carefully turned out genial man, was quick to confirm that, yes, he and his neighbours had had problems with elephants. 'They come when the crops are ripe – they are no trouble in winter. We try to chase them away by hanging cans but that no longer works – now they chase us. I like the idea of a

park. To keep the animals in one place is good; we must have our place. Some of my neighbours hate the elephants. They say to the scouts – these are your cattle, you must pay for their damage.'

'There used to be kudu here but now they're all gone and we miss them. My children have never seen a kudu. Once, when I heard that elephants were moving across open country, I took my whole family to see them. Our wives still teach the children about the wild things that remain.'

Unfortunately, Mhlongo's attitude does not prevail – not yet anyway. Many Blacks are cynical and openly dismissive of belated attempts to include them in the national conservation effort – and with good reason. As one Zulu tribesman observed, 'You Whites are strange people. You push us aside. You kill all the animals. Now you say we must put back the animals that were killed. Now, when it is late afternoon . . . I remember when the plains of my country were full of game. Then the Whites said that the nagana fly must be killed. The fly could only live on game, they said, so they sent for Whites from all over South Africa to kill the game on my plains, and there was a terrible slaughter, with hunting parties everywhere, trampling on our fields, shooting, shooting, shooting. It is puzzling to those who witnessed these killings to see a black man jailed for five years for killing one wild animal . . .' Such insensate slaughter and perverse law enforcement has made it all the harder to wean the local people away from contempt for wildlife conservation, which is a matter of education and not culture.

The next morning I was brought up-to-date on the latest developments affecting the proposed elephant reserve by Ed Ostrosky, the area ranger. We made our way down a rough, narrow track on course for Fomothini Pool – a favourite elephant waterhole – in the heart of the Mozi swamp. A hide had been built in a tree overlooking the pool as it is the best and, not incidentally, the safest way to see the elephants which, because of their harassment by man, are more likely to

charge with deadly intent than are those in more tranquil parts. As a result they have locally earned for themselves the almost mystical notoriety of the East African 'rogues' and 'shamba raiders' of old. And, as Ed pointed out with a sweep of his arm, 'In this type of country, when you first become aware of an elephant, the bloody thing's already too close.'

I would soon see what he was talking about. We were labouring through some of the thickest bush I had ever entered because driving through it in no way conveyed just how hostile it was. During my stay at Fomothini I undertook several foot patrols and it was only then, in the clutching thorn thickets, the loose sand undermining each step with no relief from the breathless trapped air, that the overwhelming aridity and unrelenting nature of the place revealed itself.

Yet, as I was to find out, for those who make their home there, who are privy to the secrets of the forest, conditions are, if not sumptuous, at least tolerable. Thonga hunters and elephants alike relieve their thirst by resorting to sip-wells of water trapped in the rot holes of trees. Enough water always remains for the hunters as the small size of the hole prevents an elephant's trunk from reaching all the way down. The people who live there are largely self sufficient. There are wild spinaches and mushrooms to be collected and wild fruits such as marulas, monkey-apples, milkberries, wild custard apples, Zulu podberries and Galla plums. In the summer they harvest marula caterpillars and are partial to a large black pomerine ant as well as the more usual fare of small antelopes, hares and ground birds. Although the age of the hunter-gatherer has passed and will never return, these pastoral Thongas, to a remarkable extent, mirror the old ways of their forebears.

My guide and companion for my stay at Fomothini was Msuthu John Ndlovu,

a newly-recruited rather apprehensive scout. Once my gear was stowed and the rest of the party had departed, I left him to build a fire while I walked down to the pool's edge to get better acquainted with my new surroundings. Dense acacia and lala palm thickets gave way to reedbeds and bullrushes that crowded the dark still saline swamp. Arch-backed fiery dragonflies skidded across the water's smooth surface in a silence so deep I could hear the dry rustle of their translucent wings. One or another would momentarily touch down to deposit her eggs, setting off a quickly extinguished ripple of concentric circles. The air pulsated with a feeling of waiting that was

Jellyfish, opposite, abound at Khosi Bay. A Thonga tribeswoman takes advantage of the low tide to hack loose mussels, limpets and other shellfish from the exposed rocks. In the wild undeveloped bay area of northern Tongaland, the indigenous people still live off the land to a remarkable extent. Above. Thonga 'sangomas' or diviners near Manguzi in Tongaland.

On the road to Sihangwane children gather around any visitor to the area, staring with wide open curiosity and all the time in the world to indulge it.

In the unspoilt Mozi swamp and dry sand forests of Sihangwane live Zululand's only surviving elephant population. Their numbers fluctuate between 75 and 150 as the free-ranging herds migrate across international borders into Moçambique and back. Fortunately, plans are advanced to establish the Tembe Elephant Reserve and so resolve the conflict that exists between agricultural tribesfolk and marauding elephants.

intensified by the apprehended presence of elephants – their signs were everywhere. I was content to bask in that special pleasure I take from visiting remote places when, from near at hand, there came a CRACK! sharp as a gunshot, as a feeding elephant demolished a tree. Just that, nothing more; the silence that followed shrieked with anticipation but the animal remained hidden.

It was not until some hours later that I actually saw my first elephant. After mid-morning tea and biscuits I indicated to Msuthu that an energizing walk would be just the thing. He received my suggestion with undisguised lack of enthusiasm but, after a moment's hesitation, glumly shrugged and set off.

We picked our way along densely overgrown elephant paths, much of the time bent double. I followed like a beacon the flash of orange where my guide's underpants showed through a rent in his coveralls, hanging back far enough to avoid the lash of his deflected branches. We periodically stopped to unhook ourselves from needle-sharp thorns or to catch our breath. At one point I spotted a thick-waisted land monitor impassively observing us from the flickering shade of a peeling commiphora. Bright points of light glowed in its hard, agate eyes; its forked tongue darted, sensuously probing. In mime I asked if the giant lizard was good to eat. Msuthu shook his head although I knew that in other parts of Africa it is considered a delicacy.

In an open field adjoining the Mozi channel we came upon a herd of sleekly rounded cattle – Nguni hybrids – collected on a green flush of new grass that had erupted in the wake of a recent burn. The stunted, symmetrically patterned cattle grazing between heaps of strewn elephant dung suggested an earlier era, before there was ever a need to protect nature by ordinance, when wild beasts shared the earth with wild man and his herds. The spoor of elephants, cattle and barefoot herdsmen have lightly marked the crust of this continent through the millennia: set amongst them, the imprint of my boot looked oppressive and alien.

We returned by a different route, not nearly as closed as the one that took us there. Distinctive, silver-leafed *Terminalia sericeas* were elegantly prominent in the green and grey forest. A pair of broadbills called unmusically back and forth to each other, both repeating the same little scale that sounded like an abbreviated trumpet score. Suddenly there on the trail before us we saw a litter of elephant droppings – steamingly fresh. Excited flies gathered; a single dung beetle droned in. The scout peered anxiously about him, speculatively nudging a dungball with the toe of his tattered blue sneaker, as if divining the elephants' whereabouts. We both knew it was close but in the enveloping forest it was impossible to see more than a few paces ahead.

Msuthu started cautiously forward, rounded a bush then froze, seeming to shrink into himself. We stood transfixed, then Msuthu wheeled and bolted past me, muttering 'elephant!'. I chased after him – under these conditions it is safest to assume the worst and put as much distance between one's self and a dangerous animal as possible. But when I didn't hear the crashing of an elephant in pursuit I pulled up, just in time to hear its heavy body moving unhurriedly away. We had been downwind so it could not have scented us and probably was only mildly disturbed by the noise of our retreat.

Of my guide there was no sign. When eventually he responded to my whistles and reappeared I flashed him a grin in a spirit of camaradie at our shared experience. Obviously though he did not regard it as a grinning matter for he simply stared at me, stony-faced, then, standing on tiptoe and stretching his hand as far above his head as he could, tried to impress upon me the enormity of the creature from which we had escaped. There was no cajoling him out of it, he was badly shaken. And perhaps his reaction was more realistic than mine – I regarded the encounter as no more than a minor adventure.

Further along we discovered a ruined and abandoned thatch hut. It was strategically sited beside a monkey-apple tree – useful both as food and shade – but which must act as a powerful magnet for any elephants in the area. A little earlier we had found cans and giant snail shells wired together and strung from branches along the trail to rattle warning of an elephant's approach. An iron bar suspen-

A Thonga pastoralist's kraal abandoned when he lost a war of nerves with raiding elephants. The iron bar suspended from a branch and a rusty file lying under it told how the herdsman had clanged away once his early warning system – cans and the shells of giant land snails hung along the trail to warn of an approaching elephant – had gone off. The fruit of the monkey-apple tree growing near the kraal must have acted as a magnet to local elephants. Far right, an elephant at Fomothini pool.

ded near the hut and a rusty file lying under it told how the herdsman had obviously clanged away once his early-warning system had gone off. But it was the elephants that had won the war of nerves; the people had given up and moved away.

Back at camp we prepared for the night. We used the clear brackish swamp water, with a measure of Dettol added as a precaution against bilharzia, to wash ourselves. After an early, simple meal we climbed into the hide just as two elephant bulls emerged from the forest for a late afternoon drink. From the safety of the hide, Msuthu could enjoy elephants well enough, exclaiming in awed undertones at their hugeness and power but it was their nonchalant demonstrations of strength that astonished, perhaps even appalled him the most. His 'Auw!' went high with incredulity when one casually ripped a branch from a tree. Through his eyes I gradually began to see these elephants in an altogether different light. What I regarded as an increasingly obsolete, almost wistfully vulnerable masterpiece appeared to

the scout, not long from one of the fragile villages, as a sinister and unfriendly force, dangerous and implacable.

Towards sunset that evening flocks of glossy starlings gathered into a teeming noisy mob at a favourite roost nearby; suddenly rising into the air as a current of alarm passed through them, then realighting with much flurrying of feathers. Their chirring and fidgeting did not cease until last light had gone from the sky and deep night closed in.

Without warning the weather turned, a wind came up, palm fronds clattered. Our hide-cum-treehouse rolled like a ship on a turbulent sea. The wind dispersed the clouds and the stars were revealed as they convened in the cosmos. A chorus of frogs throbbed throughout the night; an eagle owl called, as did despairing galagos. Towards midnight a small herd of elephants churned Fomothini's dark waters, blowing and sighing, and from time to time they echoed the hollow smack of tusk against tusk as young bulls wrestled.

The following morning Msuthu again led the way. I hoped that he would un-

derstand from my obvious interest in the deserted pastoralist's kraal that a find of a similar nature would be appreciated. Strangely though, with perverse fascination, he headed straight for the place where the day before he had confronted his nemesis and turned tail to run. Once there he peered about in fearful expectation. When nothing happened he visibly relaxed and for the first time broke into a broad smile, so delighted was he with the outcome of his defiant gesture. Then he signalled that we could return, having again tempted the Fates and survived.

On my last day at Fomothini I waited amongst the reeds at the water's edge for the vehicle to collect us. It was out of a reed, according to Zulu legend, that man and animals came. The Great Great-One made the reed to open and they stepped forth. It might well have happened here – the components were perfect to nurture new life.

As I sat there sun fired the wings of a dragonfly probing the bank's shaded overhang. Adept as the dragonfly, a pied kingfisher, its wings a blur of motion, hovered above the swamp's refractive surface, then tipped over and dropped straight down, plunging into the water with a reverberating splash. A second later it re-emerged, without a catch, but, with an optimistic chirp climbed again to seek another target. At my foot, on a cushion of leaf mould, lay a set of butterfly wings, paired as neatly and carefully as if placed in a display cabinet –

only the thorax was missing, surgically excised by a predatory bird.

The water lured all the birds in the district and the broken, overgrown nature of the place provided sanctuary and lent an air of confidence to their comings and goings. Flocks of starlings, red-billed helmet shrikes and an assortment of doves with individual nicators, square-tailed drongos and a single bearded robin arrived in a hurry, drank, and departed just as precipitously. The persistent rhythmic tapping of a superb golden-tailed woodpecker probing perished bark in search of insect larvae combined with winter warmth to induce a pleasant drowsiness that was hard to resist.

My feeling of wellbeing in these surroundings put me in mind of the secret places of my childhood, to which only my dog Kerry was invited. Then too there had been thick bush and water and the scurry of birds and small rodents. Kerry would stare up at me with quick pants of excitement, waiting my command to ferret them out. But I acted the spoilsport, taking a restraining grasp on his scruff until he subsided with small whines of frustration. He was a creature of the bush and that's how I remember him. Although he came with us when we moved to the city he couldn't adapt. He died on the street, under a car, confused and out of his environment, reacting to instincts that no longer held true. I wonder if my fate will be so very different – or yours – times are changing so fast.

BIBLIOGRAPHY

Anderson, J.L. *The Social Organisation and Aspects of Behaviour of the Nyala*. PhD. Thesis. 1978.

Ardrey, Robert. *Territorial Imperative*. Wm. Collins and Son. London. 1967.

Aves. *Red Data Book*. 1976.

Baldwin, William Charles. *African Hunting and Adventure from 1852-1860*. London. 1894.

Berruti, A. *Status and Review of Waterbirds Breeding at Lake St. Lucia*. The Lammergeyer No. 28. 1980.

Bourquin, O.; Vincent, John and Hitchins, P.M. *The Vertebrates of the Hluhluwe Game Reserve – Corridor (State Land) – Umfolozi Game Reserve Complex*. The Lammergeyer No. 14. 1971.

Bruton, M.N. and Cooper, K.H. *Studies on the Ecology of Maputaland*. Rhodes University Publication. 1980.

Bryant, A.T. *Olden Times in Zululand and Natal*. Pietermaritzburg. 1939.

Bryant, A.T. *The Zulu People – As They were before the White Man Came*. Pietermaritzburg. 1949.

Bulpin, T.V. *Shaka's Country – A Book of Zululand*. London. 1952.

Burchell, William J. *Travels in the Interior of Southern Africa*. London. 1824.

Cope, Jack. *Penguin Book of South African Verse*. Witwatersrand University Press. 1968.

Dixon, J.E.W. *Notes on Horned Female Impala*. The Lammergeyer No. 8. 1968.

Dugmore, A. Radclyffe. *Camera Adventures in the African Wilds*. London. 1910.

Dunn, John. *Cetywayo and the Three Generals*. Natal Printing Press. 1886.

Drummond, W.H. *The Large Game and Natural History of South and South East Africa*. London. 1875.

Emery, Frank. *The Red Soldier*. London. 1977.

Emslie, R.H. *Habitat Use and the Grazing Impact of the White Rhinoceros in Umfolozi Game Reserve*. Internal Report. 1982.

Findlay, F.R.N. *Big Game Shooting and Travel in South East Africa*. London. 1903.

Gardiner, A. *Narrative of a Journey to the Zoolu Country*. London. 1836.

Hall, Martin. *The Umfolozi, Hluhluwe and Corridor during the Iron Age*. The Lammergeyer No. 27. 1979.

Hall-Martin, Anthony. *Black Rhinoceros in Southern Africa*. Oryx. Vol. 15. 1979.

Hanks, J. *African Wildlife magazines*. Vol. 30. No. 2 and Vol. 34. No. 5. 1980.

Hanks, J. *A New Philosophy for Nature Conservation*. University of Natal Press. 1981.

Hanks, J. *Ecosystem Development – A New Environmental Order*. University of Natal Press. 1979.

Harris, R.H.T.P. *Report on Bionomics of Tsetse Fly*. Internal Report. Pietermaritzburg. 1937.

Harris, W. Cornwallis. *Portraits of Game and Wild Animals of Southern Africa*. London. 1840 and Facsimile A.A. Balkema. 1969.

Henkel, J.S. *Report on the Ecology of Hluhluwe Game Reserve*. Internal Report. Pietermaritzburg. 1937.

Hillman, Kes and Martin, Esmond. *Will Poaching Exterminate Kenya's Rhinos?* Oryx Vol. 15. 1979.

Hitchins, P.M. *The Status of the Black Rhinoceros in the Zululand Game and Nature Reserves*. Internal Report. 1976.

Holden, William C. *The Past and Future of the Kaffir Races*. W. Struik's Facsimile. 1963.

Hughes, G.R. *The Sea Turtles of South East Africa*. Vol. 1 and 2. *Reports for Oceanographic Research Institute*. Durban. 1974.

Isaacs, Nathaniel. *Travels and Adventures in Eastern Africa*. London. 1836.

King, L.C. *Notes on the Natural History of Nhlonhlela Hill*. Natal Parks Board Publication. 1974.

Klingelhoeffer, E.W. *Recommendation for the Proposed Tembe Elephant Reserve*. Internal Report for KwaZulu Bureau of Natural Resources. 1982.

Kolbe, F.F. *The Status of the Tsetse flies in relation to game conservation and utilization*. Journal of the S.A. Wildlife Management Association. Vol. 14. No. 1. 1974.

Krige, Uys. *Penguin Book of South African Verse*. Witwatersrand University Press. 1968.

Leslie, David. *Among the Zulus and the Amatongas*. Glasgow. 1875.

Lugg, H.C. *Life Under a Zulu Shield*. Pietermaritzburg. 1975.

Mentis, M. *Estimates of Natural Biomasses of Large Herbivores in the Umfolozi Game Reserve Area*. Internal Report. 1977.

Moll, E.J. *Plant Ecology of Mkuzi Game Reserve*. Natal Parks Board Publication. 1974.

Morris, Donald Robert. *Washing of the Spears*. Sphere. London. 1973.

Myers, Norman. *The Sinking Ark*. Oxford. 1979.

Owen-Smith, R.N. *The Behavioural Ecology of the White Rhinoceros*. PhD. Thesis. University of the Witwatersrand. 1975.

Player, Ian. *The White Rhino Saga*. London. 1972.

Player, I.C. and Feeley, J.M. *A Preliminary Report on the Square-lipped Rhinoceros*. The Lammergeyer No. 1. 1960.

Pooley, A.C. *The Status of the Nile Crocodile in the R.S.A.* Internal Report for Natal Parks Board. 1977.

Ritter, E.A. *Shaka Zulu*. London. 1955.

Samuelson, L.H. *Zululand: Its Traditions, Legends, Customs and Folklore*. Marianhill Mission Press. 1974.

Selous, F.C. *African Nature Notes and Reminiscences*. London. 1908.

Steele, Nick. *Bushlife of a Game Warden*. Pietermaritzburg. 1980.

Steele, N.A. *A Preliminary Report on the Lions in the Umfolozi and Hluhluwe Game Reserves*. Internal Report for Natal Parks Board. 1975.

Stutterheim, C.J. *Symbiont Selection of Redbilled Oxpecker in the Hluhluwe-Umfolozi Game Reserve Complex*. The Lammergeyer. 1980.

Tinley, K. and van Riet, W. *Proposals Towards an Environmental Plan for KwaZulu*. Unpublished report for the Department of Co-operation and Development. 1981.

Vincent, John. *The History of Umfolozi Game Reserve as it relates to management*. The Lammergeyer No. 11. 1970.

Vilakazi, B.W. *I Heard the Old Songs*. Edited by Jack Cope and Uys Krige. Chapter 2. 1968.

Vlahos, Olivia. *African Beginnings*. Viking. 1967.

Waterbuck bull, Umfolozi

Caracal

INDEX